Preparing for the
New Jersey
HSPA
Language Arts Literacy

Steven L. Stern

AMSCO SCHOOL PUBLICATIONS, INC.
315 Hudson Street, New York, NY 10013

Please visit our Web site at:

www.amscopub.com

THIS BOOK IS DEDICATED TO
*Doron, Sherry, Elana, Benjamin, and
Daniella.*
Thanks for sharing so much love and laughter.

Cover Design: Merrill Haber

Text Design: Merrill Haber

Text Illustration: Tony D' Adamo

Compositor: Northeastern Graphic Services

When ordering this book, please specify: *either* **R 725 W** *or*
PREPARING FOR THE NEW JERSEY HSPA IN LANGUAGE
ARTS LITERACY

ISBN 1-56765-084-8

ABOUT THE AUTHOR

Steven L. Stern has over 30 years of experience as a writer and textbook editor, developing a wide range of books, educational products, and informational materials for children and adults. He has written five other high school test-preparation books and is the author of two novels as well as numerous articles and short stories. He has also worked as an English teacher, a lexicographer, and a writing consultant.

ABOUT THE CONSULTANTS

Cynthia Baumgartner has been an English educator for 29 years and has taught in schools in New York City as well as Northern and Central New Jersey. She has served as an English Chairperson at Kearny High School in Kearny, New Jersey, supervising English, ESL, and basic skills programs. Presently, she is the English Supervisor at Howell High School in Farmingdale, New Jersey, where she has successfully initiated across-the-curriculum instruction to raise the HSPT scores in both reading and writing.

Gary Pankiewicz is a high school English and journalism teacher for grades 9–12 at Hasbrouck Heights High School in Bergen County, New Jersey. He has received the Governor's Teaching Award in his school district for his dedicated teaching practices. Mr. Pankiewicz graduated from Montclair State University with a Bachelor's degree in English. He has returned to MSU to pursue a Master's in English with a concentration in Writing Studies.

Maria Salinas has served as the Camden City's Supervisor of Language Arts for the past 20 years. She has taught undergraduate and graduate courses in language and literature at Camden County College and at Rowan University. She has served on numerous committees that center on assessment of pupil achievement in language and writing for inner city children and provided leadership in curriculum development for language arts instruction. Ms. Salinas is an active member of the National Teachers of English and has served as a teacher of English, Spanish, and English as a Second Language, and Bilingual Education.

ACKNOWLEDGMENTS

"Only Daughter," copyright © 1990 by Sandra Cisneros. First published in GLAMOUR, November 1990. Reprinted by permission of **Susan Bergholz Literary Services,** New York. All rights reserved. (page 65)

"Anxiety: Challenge by Another Name." **James Lincoln Collier,** by permission of the author. (page 191)

PHOTO CREDITS

CONTENTS

C H A P T E R 1

THE HIGH SCHOOL PROFICIENCY ASSESSMENT (HSPA) IN LANGUAGE ARTS LITERACY

1.1 Overview of the Exam
1.2 Using This Book

Reading books, magazines, and newspapers.

Writing essays and papers.

Listening to what people say.

Viewing TV programs and videos.

Speaking to other people.

Such activities play an important part in your life, both in and out of school. They all require a combination of thinking and communication skills—*language arts* skills.

The purpose of New Jersey's High School Proficiency Assessment (HSPA) in Language Arts Literacy is to test your language arts skills. Specifically, the Language Arts HSPA focuses on your ability to read with understanding and to organize and express your ideas clearly in writing.

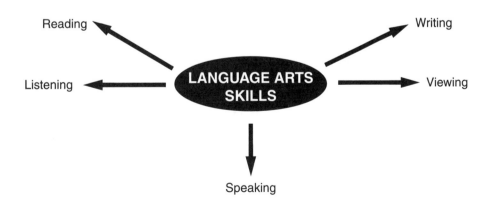

Preparing for the New Jersey HSPA in Language Arts Literacy will help you get ready for the exam by showing you exactly what to expect, sharpening the skills you'll need to do well, and giving you practice in applying these skills.

Chapter 1 presents an overview of the Language Arts HSPA and describes the organization and features of this book.

THE LANGUAGE ARTS HSPA

The HSPA is a long exam with five parts. However, you won't have to take the whole test in one day. You'll take three parts of it on one day, the remaining parts the next day.

The exam consists of various tasks. These tasks will call upon your skills in related areas of language arts:

- reading
- writing
- answering multiple-choice questions
- answering open-ended questions
- editing/revising text

Study the chart below. You'll learn about each of these tasks in the other chapters of this book.

☑ HSPA READING AND WRITING TASKS

Part 1:	Write an extended response about a picture.
Part 2:	Read a persuasive selection and answer multiple-choice and open-ended questions.
Part 3:	Revise and edit a given student essay.
Part 4:	Read a narrative selection and answer multiple-choice and open-ended questions.
Part 5:	Write a persuasive essay or letter.

Notice that the exam requires you to answer *open-ended questions* and write *extended responses*. For a definition of these important terms, see the box on page 4.

"Holistic" Scoring: Looking at the Whole

Scoring your work on the Language Arts HSPA is more complex than grading most other tests. Except for the multiple-choice questions, your work will be scored *holistically* on the basis of specific pre-set criteria, or standards. Holistic scoring means that the criteria will all be applied together, simultaneously.

In other words, for each writing activity of the HSPA, your work will be viewed *as a whole*. Scorers will form an impression by considering all the criteria at the same time, weighing them equally, and arriving at a single score.

You won't earn points for doing one thing or lose points for doing something else. Instead, scorers will consider the overall effectiveness of your work on the particular task.

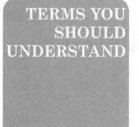

An **open-ended question** asks you to reflect on a selection and then write a thoughtful answer that shows your insight into the selection. Your answer is based on your understanding of the text and your knowledge of the elements and structure of fiction and nonfiction. Open-ended questions are discussed in detail in Chapter 2.

A **prompt** consists of directions and information explaining exactly what you have to do for part of a test. For example, Parts 1 and 5 of the HSPA have writing prompts.

An **extended response** is an essay, letter, or other multiple-paragraph composition that you write in response to a prompt. Extended responses are discussed in detail in Chapter 4.

 ## Scoring Guides, or "Rubrics"

For individual parts of the HSPA, scorers will use specific scoring *rubrics*. A rubric is a set of detailed descriptive guidelines that helps scorers determine the appropriate score. Scorers will refer to one rubric for grading open-ended questions, another for extended responses, and a third for the revise/edit task.

Rubrics help scorers evaluate your work as a whole. For example, content, organization, and other elements of writing must all work together in order for a writer to communicate effectively. A holistic scoring rubric emphasizes the combination and blending of these elements.

Activity: Understanding the Exam

You've read that the Language Arts HSPA tests your skills in related areas of language arts. Summarize how the exam does this.

_____

_____

_____

_____

_____

_____

_____

_____

_____

_____

1.2 USING THIS BOOK

CONTENT AND ORGANIZATION

This book is organized into four chapters, and each chapter is divided into sections.

- Chapter 1, which you're reading now, introduces the Language Arts HSPA exam and gives an overview of the content and features of this book.

- Chapter 2 discusses the kinds of selections you'll find on the HSPA and provides strategies for answering the multiple-choice and open-ended questions. Chapter 2 has three sections:
  - **2.1** Selections and Questions
  - **2.2** Multiple-Choice Questions
  - **2.3** Open-Ended Questions

- Chapter 3 focuses on language arts skills you'll need to apply to the HSPA reading selections. Chapter 3 has five sections:
  - **3.1** Identifying Important Ideas and Information
  - **3.2** Making Inferences and Drawing Conclusions
  - **3.3** Using Context to Determine Meaning
  - **3.4** Understanding an Author's Purpose and Point of View
  - **3.5** Examining Elements of Fiction and Nonfiction

- Chapter 4 deals with the writing tasks that appear on the HSPA. This chapter has four sections:
  - **4.1** HSPA Writing Tasks
  - **4.2** Extended Response: Writing About a Picture
  - **4.3** Extended Response: Writing to Persuade
  - **4.4** The Revise/Edit Task

- Two complete practice tests follow Chapter 4.

FEATURES

To cover a wide range of content in a comprehensive yet easy-to-understand way, this book contains many helpful features. For example, strategies appear in dark type for ready reference and review. Lists and diagrams emphasize or clarify important information. Other features include the following:

- **Activities.** Various activities throughout the book provide practice and reinforcement of what you learn. Most activities are intended for independent work. A few involve working with a partner or a small group of students.
- ***Applying Your Knowledge*** and ***Thinking It Through.*** These related sections first give you an opportunity to try out what you've

learned and then lead you step-by-step through the thought processes involved in arriving at the correct answers.

- **Writing models**. Sample plans and responses based on the plans illustrate how to respond effectively to prompts.
- *FYI* (For Your Information). These boxes appear throughout the book, providing useful information and tips for doing your best on the exam.
- **Boxed features**. Certain basic information is highlighted in separate boxes. For example, you'll see one box describing methods of organization, another explaining ways to distinguish fact from opinion.
- *Review* **summaries**. Brief summaries of key strategies and concepts appear at the end of Chapter 2 and at the end of each section of Chapters 3 and 4.
- **Practice test items**. Two complete practice tests appear after Chapter 4. In addition, practice test items and activities appear at the end of Chapter 2 and at the end of each section of Chapters 3 and 4.

HSPA MULTIPLE-CHOICE AND OPEN-ENDED QUESTIONS

2.1 Selections and Questions
2.2 Multiple-Choice Questions
2.3 Open-Ended Questions
Feature: *Topic Sentences for Open-Ended Questions*
Feature: *Using Quotation Marks*

Each day you come across a wide range of printed and visual materials. These materials generally fall into the following categories, depending on content and purpose:

NARRATIVE writing tells a story. Novels and short stories are examples of narrative writing.

PERSUASIVE writing tries to influence how you think or act. Editorials, political speeches, and movie reviews are examples of persuasive writing.

INFORMATIONAL writing communicates information. Textbooks, news magazines, and reference books contain informational text.

Of course, written works often fit in more than just one category. For example, the content of a magazine article may be both persuasive and informational. A narrative work may include facts about real events and places.

The Language Arts HSPA contains a narrative selection and a persuasive selection. Each selection is followed by ten multiple-choice and two open-ended questions. These questions test your understanding of the text as well as your knowledge of the elements and structure of fiction and nonfiction works.

The strategies discussed in this chapter will help you do your best on the HSPA tasks highlighted below.

☑ **HSPA READING AND WRITING TASKS**

	Part 1:	Write an extended response about a picture.
✔	**Part 2:**	Read a persuasive selection and answer multiple-choice and open-ended questions.
	Part 3:	Revise and edit a given student essay.
✔	**Part 4:**	Read a narrative selection and answer multiple-choice and open-ended questions.
	Part 5:	Write a persuasive essay or letter.

The HSPA reading selections may be complete pieces or excerpts from longer works. For example, the persuasive selection for Part 2 of the exam could be an essay in defense of computer games or an editorial calling for an increase in the minimum wage. The narrative selection for Part 4 could be a short story or an excerpt from a novel.

To get an idea of what the Language Arts HSPA looks like, examine the sample test item below. **Just glance over it quickly for now. You'll have a chance to read the selection and answer the multiple-choice and open-ended questions later in this chapter.**

The word *addiction* is usually associated with drug abuse. However, in this excerpt from her book *The Plug-In Drug*, the author presents her views on a different sort of addiction.

Television Addiction
by Marie Winn

Cookies or Heroin?

The word "addiction" is often used loosely and wryly in conversation. People will refer to themselves as "mystery book addicts" or "cookie addicts." E. B. White wrote of his annual surge of interest in gardening: "We are hooked and are making an attempt to kick the habit." Yet nobody really believes that reading mysteries or ordering seeds by catalogue is serious enough to be compared with addictions to heroin or alcohol. The word "addiction" is here used jokingly to denote a tendency to overindulge in some pleasurable activity.

People often refer to being "hooked on TV." Does this, too, fall into the lighthearted category of cookie eating and other pleasures that people pursue with unusual intensity, or is there a kind of television viewing that falls into the more serious category of destructive addiction?

When we think about addiction to drugs or alcohol we frequently focus on negative aspects, ignoring the plea- sures that accompany drinking or drug-taking. And yet the essence of any serious addiction is a pursuit of pleasure, a search for a "high" that normal life does not supply. It is only the inability to function without the addictive substance that is dismaying, the dependence of the organism upon a certain experience and an increasing inability to function normally without it. Thus people will take two or three drinks at the end of the day not merely for the pleasure drinking provides, but also because they "don't feel normal" without them.

Real addicts do not merely pursue a pleasurable experience one time in order to function normally. They need to *repeat* it again and again. Something about that particular experience makes life without it less than complete. Other potentially pleasurable experiences are no longer possible, for under the spell of the addictive experience, their lives are peculiarly distorted. The addict craves an experience and yet he is never really satisfied. The organism may be temporarily <u>sated</u>, but soon it begins to crave again.

Finally a serious addiction is distinguished from a harmless pursuit of pleasure by its distinctly destructive ele-

4

5

ments. Heroin addicts, for instance, lead a damaged life: their increasing need for heroin in increasing doses prevents them from working, from maintaining relationships, from developing in human ways. Similarly alcoholics' lives are narrowed and dehumanized by their dependence on alcohol.

Let us consider television viewing in the light of the conditions that define serious addictions.

Not unlike drugs or alcohol, the television experience allows the participant to blot out the real world and enter into a pleasurable and passive mental state. The worries and anxieties of reality are as effectively deferred by becoming absorbed in a television program as by going on a "trip" induced by drugs or alcohol. And just as alcoholics are only vaguely aware of their addiction, feeling that they control their drinking more than they really do **7** ("I can cut it out any time I want—I just like to have three or four drinks before dinner"), people similarly overestimate their control over television watching. Even as they put off other activities to spend hour after hour watching television, they feel they could easily resume living in a different, less passive style. But somehow or other, while the television set is present in their homes, the click doesn't sound. With television pleasures available, those other experiences seem less attractive, more difficult somehow.

A heavy viewer (a college English instructor) observes: "I find television almost irresistible. When the set is on, I cannot ignore it. I can't turn it off. I feel sapped, will-less, enervated. As I reach out to turn off the set, the strength goes out of my arms. So I sit there for hours and hours."

Self-confessed television addicts often feel they "ought" to do other things—but the fact that they don't read and don't plant their garden or sew or crochet or play games or have conversations means that those activities are no longer as desirable as television viewing. In a way the lives of heavy viewers are as imbalanced by their television "habit" as a drug addict's or an alcoholic's. They are **9** living in a holding pattern, as it were, passing up the activities that lead to growth or development or a sense of accomplishment. This is one reason people talk about their television viewing so ruefully, so apologetically. They are aware that it is an unproductive experience, that almost any other endeavor is more worthwhile by any human measure.

Finally it is the <u>adverse</u> effect of television viewing on the lives of so many people that defines it as a serious addiction. The television habit distorts the sense of time. It renders other experiences vague and curiously unreal while **10** taking on a greater reality for itself. It weakens relationships by reducing and sometimes eliminating normal opportunities for talking, for communicating.

And yet television does not satisfy, else why would the viewer continue to watch hour after hour, day after day? "The measure of health," writes Lawrence Kubie, "is flexibility . . . and especially the freedom to cease when **11** sated." But heavy television viewers can never be sated with their television experiences—these do not provide the true nourishment that satiation requires—and thus they find that they cannot stop watching.

1. The word **sated** in paragraph 4 means

    A. confused.
    B. sleepy.
    C. satisfied.
    D. nervous.

2. To effectively get her point across, the author

    A. organizes her facts and details chronologically.
    B. includes quotations from heroin addicts.
    C. first defines the conditions of addiction, then tells how TV viewing meets these conditions.
    D. clearly states her central idea in the opening paragraph.

3. When the author writes that "worries and anxieties of reality are . . . effectively deferred by becoming absorbed in a television program" (paragraph 7), she means that

    A. viewers temporarily escape their troubles.
    B. television helps viewers solve their problems.
    C. high-quality television is good for viewers' health.
    D. viewers can improve their lives through television.

4. Which statement BEST expresses the central idea of the selection?

    A. Television viewers should be more selective in what they watch.
    B. Watching television can become a serious addiction.

C. Many television viewers become drug addicts.

D. There are both positive and negative aspects to watching television.

5. In paragraph 9, the author writes, "He is living in a holding pattern, as it were, passing up the activities that lead to growth or development or a sense of accomplishment." Which of the following positions does this statement support?

A. Television addicts have something in common with drug addicts.

B. Most television viewers are by nature lazy people with little ambition.

C. People who watch television generally lead active lives.

D. Heavy viewers don't realize they have a problem.

6. The author's tone can best be described as

A. distant and amused.

B. puzzled and sympathetic.

C. sad and uncertain.

D. serious and concerned.

7. The word **adverse** as it is used in paragraph 10 means

A. harmful.

B. exciting.

C. positive.

D. insignificant.

8. According to the author, each of the following is a defining characteristic of serious addiction EXCEPT

A. destructive effects.

B. the ability to stop at any time.

C. pleasurable feelings.

D. the need to repeat the experience.

9. With which of the following statements would the author most likely agree?

A. Being addicted to TV is no worse than being addicted to mystery novels or gardening.

B. The problem of people being "hooked on TV" should not be taken lightly.

C. TV addiction would not be a concern if the quality of programs was higher.

D. Addiction to TV is more dangerous than addiction to heroin.

10. In paragraph 11, the author writes, "And yet television does not satisfy, else why would the viewer continue to watch hour after hour, day after day?" This is an example of

A. symbolism.

B. a rhetorical question.

C. understatement.

D. figurative language.

OPEN-ENDED ITEMS

11. In paragraph 5, the author states that "a serious addiction is distinguished from a harmless pursuit of pleasure by its distinctly destructive elements."

• What "destructive elements" does the author associate with television viewing?

• How might a TV addict's life change if his/her addiction ended?

Use information from the selection to support your response.

_____

_____

_____

_____

_____

12. The author compares television viewing to drug and alcohol use.

• In what ways does the author see the two as similar?

• What aspect of television viewing do you think the author considers most harmful?

Use information from the selection to support your response.

_____

_____

_____

_____

_____

_____

Introductions to Selections

Each HSPA selection has a brief introduction, which sets the stage for what you're going to read. For example, the selection above has this introduction:

> **The word *addiction* is usually associated with drug abuse. However, in this excerpt from her book *The Plug-In Drug*, the author presents her views on a different sort of addiction.**

Such an introduction is helpful in several ways. It suggests what the selection is about and whether it's fiction or nonfiction. It tells whether the selection is an excerpt or a complete work. Finally, the introduction may indicate the author's purpose for writing.

Specifically, the above introduction tells you that you're going to read a book excerpt about some sort of addiction. Because the author "presents her views," you know that the piece is likely to be persuasive writing.

Activity A: Reading Introductions

Two selection introductions appear below. Read each one and answer the questions.

> **You've probably heard the old saying that "it's better to have loved and lost than never to have loved at all." The experience of the two characters in the following story may make you question whether the saying is true.**

1. What information does this introduction give you about the selection? Be specific.

    _____

    _____

    _____

> **Some people believe that success is measured by how much money you earn. In this article, the writer presents a different perspective of what truly matters in life.**

2. What information does this introduction give you about the selection? About the author's purpose for writing it? Be specific.

    _____

    _____

    _____

3. You read earlier that the introduction "sets the stage for what you're going to read." In your own words, explain what this statement means.

    _____

    _____

    _____

"Constructing Meaning"

Educators sometimes describe reading as a process through which readers *construct meaning*. What this means is that you combine what you already know with information you gain from the text in order to make sense of what you read. The HSPA questions test your ability to construct meaning.

Constructing meaning requires a variety of skills. For example, you must be able to identify the main ideas of a selection and to determine an author's purpose and point of view. You'll learn more about applying these and other reading and thinking skills in Chapter 3.

STRATEGIES FOR *ACTIVE* READING

Reading requires thought and concentration. It is an active process—a process of applying your mental skills to analyze and interpret ideas and information. The strategies that follow will help you read the HSPA selections *actively*.

> **Get information from the introduction.**
> Read the introduction with care. What does it tell you about the selection? What does it suggest about the author's purpose or point of view?

> **Think about the selection title.**
> Authors choose titles carefully. Before you read the selection, and again after you read it, think about the meaning of the title.

> **Skim the questions before you read.**
> You're reading the selection in order to answer the multiple-choice and open-ended questions that follow. So, *before* reading, take a moment to look over the questions. Skimming them beforehand will alert you to important ideas and information to watch for as you read.

> **Read carefully and thoughtfully.**
> Reflect on why the author is writing and what the author wants to communicate. Remember that some ideas may be stated, while others may only be implied. Watch for important ideas and supporting facts and details.

> **Pay attention to text features and visual aids.**
> Authors blend various text elements to communicate their ideas. Watch for headings and subheadings, **boldface** and *italic* type, charts, and illustrations. Such features and visual aids offer important clues to both the meaning and organization of selections.

> **Reread and think about difficult parts.**
> Don't be tempted to skip over parts of a selection that you don't immediately understand. Instead, take the time to reread the text— several times, if necessary—and try to grasp its meaning. Use the

context (the words that come before and after) to help you figure out the meaning of a particular word, phrase, or sentence.

➤ **Consider the author's use of literary elements and techniques.**
Ask yourself how the author goes about getting his/her ideas across. Be aware of the selection's structure and organization. Think about the various elements of fiction and nonfiction. You'll learn more about these elements in Chapter 3.

➤ **Take notes.**
Jotting down key points can help you understand what you read. The next part of this chapter contains suggestions for taking notes.

Active reading means . . .

➡ focusing complete attention on what you read

➡ thinking about an author's ideas and how he or she conveys them

➡ making note of key points as you read.

Tips for Taking Notes

While you don't *have to* take notes as you read the HSPA selections, you'll probably find doing so useful. In addition to helping you understand what you read, notes help you locate information you'll want to use when answering the multiple-choice and open-ended questions. Here are some tips:

➤ **Use a simplified outline form.**
You need not take many notes. Furthermore, the notes you do take can be much simpler than those for, say, a school assignment. What you write—and how much—is up to you. For one selection, you may want to take many notes throughout. For another, you may choose to jot down just a few phrases about particular paragraphs. Use whatever method works for you and you're comfortable with.

You can make your notes easy to follow by writing ideas at the left margin and indenting supporting information beneath them. Precede each supporting detail with a dash or a number. Here's an example:

First important idea (or particular paragraph)
  —supporting detail
  —supporting detail

Second important idea (or particular paragraph)
  —supporting detail
  —supporting detail

Leave space between ideas, in case you want to add information. Also, leave wide margins on both sides of your notes.

➤ **Keep your notes short, simple, and clear.**
Zero in on *just the most important* ideas and information. Write words and phrases, not whole sentences.

➤ **Include paragraph numbers for reference.**
You'll be looking back at the selection as you answer the questions. Noting which paragraphs contain important ideas will help you find those ideas quickly.

➤ **Note details that relate to questions you'll have to answer.**
Jot down relevant information, even when it doesn't fit in neatly with your outline. For example, suppose that an open-ended question asks you to discuss an author's feelings about a particular issue. As you read the selection, make note of such feelings and where in the selection the author expresses them.

➤ **Use shortcuts.**
Shorten words, and use abbreviations and symbols such as these:

&	and	e.g.	for example
B4	before	$	money
info	information	%	percent
w/	with	w/o	without

Also, write numerals, rather than spell out numbers.

➤ **Highlight notes that are especially important.**
Underline or circle key words, or print them in capital letters. You may also find it helpful to underline important points in the reading selection itself.

APPLYING YOUR KNOWLEDGE

Let's see how the strategies and tips you've learned can be put to use. Do the following:

1. Using the "Strategies for Active Reading" on pages 13–14, read the selection "Television Addiction" (pages 9–10). However, for the time being, don't take any notes.

2. When you've finished reading the selection, look again at the first five paragraphs, shown below. Reread these paragraphs, and compare them with the sample student notes.

3. Think about these questions:

   • Which of the note-taking tips on pages 14–15 did the student apply?
   • How are the notes organized?

- What ideas and details does the student include? Why did the student choose to include them?
- What shortcuts does the student use?

4. Read "Thinking It Through," below.

Cookies or Heroin?

The word "addiction" is often used loosely and wryly in conversation. People will refer to themselves as "mystery book addicts" or "cookie addicts." E. B. White wrote of his annual surge of interest in gardening: "We are hooked and are making an attempt to kick the habit." Yet nobody really believes that reading mysteries or ordering seeds by catalogue is serious enough to be compared with addictions to heroin or alcohol. The word "addiction" is here used jokingly to denote a tendency to overindulge in some pleasurable activity.

People often refer to being "hooked on TV." Does this, too, fall into the lighthearted category of cookie eating and other pleasures that people pursue with unusual intensity, or is there a kind of television viewing that falls into the more serious category of destructive addiction?

When we think about addiction to drugs or alcohol we frequently focus on negative aspects, ignoring the pleasures that accompany drinking or drug-taking. And yet the essence of any serious addiction is a pursuit of pleasure, a search for a "high" that normal life does not supply. It is only the inability to function without the addictive substance that is dismaying, the dependence of the organism upon a certain experience and an increasing inability to function normally without it. Thus people will take two or three drinks at the end of the day not merely for the pleasure drinking provides, but also because they "don't feel normal" without them.

Real addicts do not merely pursue a pleasurable experience one time in order to function normally. They need to *repeat* it again and again. Something about that particular experience makes life without it less than complete. Other potentially pleasurable experiences are no longer possible, for under the spell of the addictive experience, their lives are peculiarly distorted. The addict craves an experience and yet he is never really satisfied. The organism may be temporarily sated, but soon it begins to crave again.

Finally a serious addiction is distinguished from a harmless pursuit of pleasure by its distinctly destructive elements. Heroin addicts, for instance, lead a damaged life: their increasing need for heroin in increasing doses prevents them from working, from maintaining relationships, from developing in human ways. Similarly alcoholics' lives are narrowed and dehumanized by their dependence on alcohol.

STUDENT NOTES

Note: These notes are only an example. Your own notes might be organized or worded differently, and they might be more or less detailed.

Elements of serious addiction (P3)
  —*pursuit of pleasure*
  —*search for "high"*
  —*dependence on certain experience*
  —*increasing inability to function w/o it
     (e.g., drinks)*

Addiction distorts addict's life (P4)
  —*addict needs to repeat experience*
  —*craves exper. but never satis.*

Addiction vs. harmless pleasure (P5)
  —*destruc. elements*
  —*heroin addict can't work, can't maintain
     relations*
  —*alcoholic's life "narrowed & dehumanized"*

Thinking It Through

As you compare the student's notes with the selection, notice the following:

- The student chose not to take notes for every paragraph, only for those paragraphs that seemed most important or relevant.
- The notes are brief and clear. The student wrote in phrases, not sentences, and used various shortcuts. For example, the student wrote "satis." for "satisfied" and "destruc." for "destructive." The student also used the abbreviations "e.g.," "w/o," and "vs."
- The student included only the most important ideas and details. Paragraph numbers (*P3, P4*) are included for easy reference. The student underlined the phrase "needs to repeat" for emphasis.
- Skimming the questions before reading the selection helped guide the student's note-taking. For example, having read the two open-ended questions, the student was alert for references to "destructive elements" and for any mention of drug or alcohol use.

Activity B: Reading and Taking Notes

Reread the selection "Television Addiction" (pages 9–10), this time taking notes. Apply the reading strategies and note-taking tips that you've learned. For paragraphs 1–5, you can take your own notes or adapt the sample student notes on page 16.

Save your notes for later use.

Activity C: Developing Note-Taking Skills

Peer feedback. Work with a partner. Exchange the notes you took for *Activity B*, and evaluate each other's work. Be constructive and specific in your suggestions. Here are some questions to consider:

- Do the notes cover the most important and relevant ideas and details?
- Are the notes as brief and clear as they can be?
- How can the notes be made even more useful?

STRATEGIES FOR ANSWERING THE QUESTIONS

The ten multiple-choice questions that follow each of the HSPA selections test many different reading and thinking skills. To answer the questions, you'll use the strategies that you learned earlier in this chapter. In Chapter 3, you'll learn additional skills to help you analyze the selections and answer the questions.

You'll find two types of multiple-choice questions on the exam: sentence completion and question and answer. Both types offer four answer choices. Here's an example of each type:

SENTENCE COMPLETION:

At the beginning of the story, the girl laughs because

   A.   she thinks the joke is funny.

   B.   the teacher is watching her.

   C.   her friends are all laughing.

   D.   she doesn't know what else to do.

QUESTION AND ANSWER:

Which one of the following proposals does the author support?

   A.   raising the legal driving age

   B.   limiting the hours that teenagers can drive

   C.   reducing the speed limit

   D.   restricting the number of passengers that can ride with a new driver

Here are some strategies to help you answer the multiple-choice questions:

> **Make sure that you understand the *question* before you consider the answer choices.**

> **Identify key words in questions.**
> For example, in the following question, the word *best* is a key word. It cautions you to look for the descriptive word that is *most* appropriate:

> > The mood of this story can <u>best</u> be described as. . .

> Key words such as *most likely* and *might* usually signal that a question is asking you to make a judgment or inference:

> > With which of the following statements would the author <u>most likely</u> agree?

> > Who <u>might</u> use this article as a basis for argument?

Key words may appear in capital letters:

What does the author enjoy MOST about his work?

Which of the following details BEST supports the position?

Some key words tell you exactly what to look for:

The <u>central idea</u> of this article. . .

The main <u>theme</u> of the story. . .

The <u>purpose</u> of daydreams in this story. . .

The <u>comparison</u> reveals. . .

An example of a <u>metaphor</u>. . .

➢ **Read and compare _all_ the choices. Then choose the best and most complete answer.**
For sentence-completion-type questions, reread the question with each possible answer. For question-and-answer-type questions, you'll often find it helpful to consider what the answer _should_ be before you look at the choices.

Watch for subtle differences between answer choices. Keep in mind that the first choice that _looks_ right may not be the _best_ choice.

➢ **Refer to the reading selection, and to your notes, as often as you need to.**

➢ **Use context to help you.**
When a question refers to a specific paragraph, review that paragraph before trying to answer. You may also need to look at the preceding or following paragraph. Remember that context clues can help you understand both stated and implied ideas. You'll learn more about using context clues in Chapter 3 (pages 80–90).

➢ **Narrow your search.**
If you're not sure which answer is correct, cross out choices you know are _in_correct. Then focus on just the remaining choices.

➢ **Don't get stuck on a difficult question.**
Make your best choice, and then move on. If you have time left over, you can return to the troublesome question. Also, you'll sometimes discover that answering one question helps you answer another.

➢ **Be sure to answer every question.**

APPLYING YOUR KNOWLEDGE

1. Review the selection "Television Addiction" (pages 9–10). Also review the notes you took for _Activity B_, on page 17.

2. Next, answer multiple-choice questions 1–10 on pages 10–11. Circle the letter next to the best answer.

3. After you've answered the questions, read "Thinking It Through" below to see how one student chose the correct answers.

Thinking It Through

1. The word **sated** in paragraph 4 means

    A. confused.
    B. sleepy.
    C. satisfied.
    D. nervous.

    To answer the question, I reread paragraph 4. I see that the word sated appears in the context of the last two sentences: The addict craves an experience and yet he is never really satisfied. The organism may be temporarily sated, but soon it begins to crave again. From this context, I can see that sated and satisfied have similar meanings. Therefore, the correct answer is choice C.

2. To effectively get her point across, the author

    A. organizes her facts and details chronologically.
    B. includes quotations from heroin addicts.
    C. first defines the conditions of addiction, then tells how TV viewing meets these conditions.
    D. clearly states her central idea in the opening paragraph.

    I believe the right answer is choice C, but I carefully read and compare all the choices. I immediately eliminate choices A and B, because they are not true. Reviewing the opening paragraph, I see that choice D also is not true. Choice C is correct.

3. When the author writes that "worries and anxieties of reality are . . . effectively deferred by becoming absorbed in a television program" (paragraph 7), she means that

    A. viewers temporarily escape their troubles.
    B. television helps viewers solve their problems.
    C. high-quality television is good for viewers' health.
    D. viewers can improve their lives through television.

    From carefully reading the selection, I know that the author's opinion of television is not a positive one. Therefore, choices B, C, and D are unlikely answers. Reviewing paragraph 7, the context tells me that choice A is the correct answer.

4. Which statement BEST expresses the central idea of the selection?

    A. Television viewers should be more selective in what they watch.
    B. Watching television can become a serious addiction.
    C. Many television viewers become drug addicts.
    D. There are both positive and negative aspects to watching television.

I pay special attention to the key words in this question: BEST and central idea. Even though the author might agree with the other statements, choice B is the best statement of the selection's central idea.

5. In paragraph 9, the author writes, "They are living in a holding pattern, as it were, passing up the activities that lead to growth or development or a sense of accomplishment." Which of the following positions does this statement support?

    A. Television addicts have something in common with drug addicts.
    B. Most television viewers are by nature lazy people with little ambition.
    C. People who watch television generally lead active lives.
    D. Heavy viewers don't realize they have a problem.

First, I read the question over to make sure that I understand it. Then I review paragraph 9 to get a sense of the whole context. The sentence ". . .a heavy viewer's life is as imbalanced . . . as a drug addict's. . ." helps me conclude that the correct answer is choice A.

6. The author's tone can best be described as

    A. distant and amused.
    B. puzzled and sympathetic.
    C. sad and uncertain.
    D. serious and concerned.

I know that "tone" is the attitude an author shows toward his or her subject. Thinking about each of the choices, I conclude that the author's tone can best be described as "serious and concerned." Choice D is the correct answer.

7. The word **adverse** as it is used in paragraph 10 means

    A. harmful.
    B. exciting.
    C. positive.
    D. insignificant.

Paragraph 10 describes various negative effects of television viewing. These effects are supporting details for the idea expressed in the paragraph's first sentence: "It is the adverse effect of television viewing. . ." From this context, I know that adverse must mean "harmful." The correct answer is choice A.

8. According to the author, each of the following is a defining characteristic of serious addiction EXCEPT

    A. destructive effects.
    B. the ability to stop at any time.

C. pleasurable feelings.

D. the need to repeat the experience.

I recognize that the word ECEPT is a key word in this question. It tells me that I have to identify the one item that is not "a defining characteristic of serious addiction." From the selection, I know that choices A, C, and D are all defining characteristics, but B is not. Therefore, choice B is the correct answer.

9. With which of the following statements would the author most likely agree?

A. Being addicted to TV is no worse than being addicted to mystery novels or gardening.

B. The problem of people being "hooked on TV" should not be taken lightly.

C. TV addiction would not be a concern if the quality of programs was higher.

D. Addiction to TV is more dangerous than addiction to heroin.

The author makes clear that she thinks television addiction is a serious matter, so choice B is probably the answer. However, I consider each of the other possibilities. Choices A and D are definitely wrong, and choice C is not supported by the selection. Therefore, choice B is correct.

10. In paragraph 11, the author writes, "And yet television does not satisfy, else why would the viewer continue to watch hour after hour, day after day?" This is an example of

A. symbolism.

B. a rhetorical question.

C. understatement.

D. figurative language.

I recognize this as a rhetorical question—a question asked only for effect or to make a statement, not to get an answer. To be sure, I consider the other choices and eliminate them. Choice B is correct.

Activity D: Improving Your Skills

Compare your responses to the multiple-choice questions with those discussed in "Thinking It Through." Then answer the following questions. Be specific.

1. (a) Which of the multiple-choice questions did you find most challenging? Why?

_____

_____

(b) What can you do to make answering such questions easier in the future?

_____

_____

2. Overall, what could you have done to improve your understanding of the selection?

_____

_____

3. Compare your answers to the preceding questions with the answers of other students. What ideas from other students might help you as well?

_____

_____

INSIGHTFUL WRITTEN RESPONSES

Open-ended questions follow each of the HSPA reading selections. These questions may touch on some of the same points that the multiple-choice questions do. However, instead of simply *choosing* an answer, for open-ended questions you'll have to *write* one. That is, you'll have to write a response that is one or more paragraphs in length.

Each open-ended item on the HSPA consists of two related questions, each one preceded by a bullet (•). You'll find various kinds of open-ended questions on the exam. Compare the examples below. What similarities and differences do you see?

EXAMPLE A:

David Scott promises that "sooner or later I will succeed, no matter what anyone thinks."

- Identify those qualities that are likely to enable David Scott to achieve his goal.
- Explain what ONE quality you think will prove most important in Scott's struggle to succeed.

Use information from the selection to support your response.

EXAMPLE B:

The experience on the beach has a significant impact on the entire family.

- How does each family member react to the experience?
- How will what happened affect each family member in the future?

Use information from the story to support your response.

EXAMPLE C:

In paragraph 6, the author advises young people to "put more effort into planning for the challenges ahead."

- To what "challenges" is the author referring?
- How might a young person's life change if he or she decided to take the author's advice?

Use information from the article to support your response.

As you can see from these examples, you'll have to think carefully about the selection before responding to an open-ended question. Open-ended questions don't ask you just to recall facts and details. Rather, they ask you to write thoughtful responses that show your insight into the selection. Note that one element common to *all* open-ended questions is that you must "use information from the selection to support your response."

To answer open-ended questions . . .

➡ write a *thoughtful* response that shows your insight into the selection

➡ *support* your response with specific ideas and details from the selection

How Open-Ended Items Are Scored

Your written responses to the open-ended items will be scored on the basis of the guidelines shown below.

SCORING GUIDELINES FOR OPEN-ENDED ITEMS

✓ Did you understand the selection?

✓ Did you understand the questions and the writing task?

✓ How clearly and effectively did you answer the questions?

✓ How much insight into the selection and the questions does your answer show?

✓ Did you adequately support your answer with ideas and details from the selection?

Note that the length of a response does not in itself affect your score. A one-paragraph response that is clearly focused and well written will score higher than a vague and rambling three-paragraph response.

Remember, too, that no one approach works for every open-ended item. For some items, you may find that a single long paragraph does the job. For other items, you may need to write two or three paragraphs to answer adequately. *Always tailor your approach to the particular question.*

Open-Ended Items: Paired Questions

Open-ended items on the HSPA generally consist of a pair of related questions. Exactly *how* the questions are related varies. For example, sometimes the second question is a direct extension of the first. Other times, the first question asks you to explain something, and the second question asks you to make an inference or prediction based on your explanation.

STRATEGIES FOR ANSWERING THE OPEN-ENDED QUESTIONS

Several of the strategies that you learned for the multiple-choice questions will also help you answer the open-ended questions. Let's see how.

> **Make sure that you understand the question.**
> Take your time. Read the open-ended item over several times. Remember that each item consists of two questions. Be sure you fully understand both questions *and* the writing task.

> **Identify key words in questions.**
> Occasionally a key word in an open-ended question appears in capital letters (like the word *ONE* in *Example A* on page 24), but usually it's up to *you* to identify key words. Here are a few tips:

> - Pay special attention to verbs. Words like *identify*, *explain*, and *predict* tell you what to do. (See *Example A* on page 24.)
> - Phrases like "you believe" and "you think" signal that a question is asking you to make a judgment. (See *Example A* on page 24.)
> - Phrases like "how might," "how would," "how could," and "how will" signal that a question is asking you to make an inference. (See *Examples B* and *C* on page 24.)

> **Use context to help you.**
> Open-ended questions often refer to specific portions of text. Always review the full context of the quoted text before answering the question.

> **Refer to the reading selection, and to your notes, as often as you need to.**
> You'll also find it useful to look back at the multiple-choice questions. Often, they will help you recall important ideas and information.

Activity E: Recognizing Key Words

Identifying key words in questions is an important strategy for answering both multiple-choice and open-ended questions. Explain why. Include specific examples to support your answer.

_____

_____

_____

_____

_____

Developing a Response

As the preceding strategies suggest, the "secret" to responding to the open-ended items on the HSPA is to *think before you write*. Your approach—within the time allowed—should be much like your approach to writing any short essay. Start by thinking about what ideas you want to get across. Then convey those ideas as clearly and effectively as you can. Here's how:

> To respond to an open-ended item . . .
>
> Step 1: Make a plan.
>
> Step 2: Write your response.
>
> Step 3: Revise/edit.
>
> Step 4: Proofread.

Let's examine each of these steps.

> ➤ **Step 1: Make a plan.**
> Begin by focusing, one at a time, on each of the questions that make up the open-ended item. Then think about how the two questions are connected. Once the questions and the writing task are clear in your mind, decide what main idea(s) you're going to base your answer on.
>
> *For some open-ended items, you'll be able to organize your response around a single main idea. However, for most open-ended items, you'll probably find it best to organize your response around two main ideas, one corresponding to each question.*
>
> Jot down your main idea. Then briefly list supporting information—specific ideas and details from the selection to support and develop your main idea. Exactly how much supporting information you'll include will depend on the selection and on the particular question.
>
> Just as when taking notes, you'll find it useful to include paragraph numbers for quick reference.

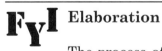 Elaboration

The process of developing an idea is called *elaboration*. Elaboration helps make writing clear and specific.

You can develop your main ideas with various kinds of information from the selection, such as:

related ideas	explanations	quotations
facts	supporting details	anecdotes
reasons	examples	
statistics	observations	

Next, number the supporting details. You can number them either in the order you plan to present them or in order of importance. You can change your mind later, but numbering the details will help you organize your thoughts.

If you're going to present more than one main idea in your response, list and number supporting information for each one.

First main idea
   ① —*supporting idea/detail*
   ② —*supporting idea/detail*

Second main idea
   ① —*supporting idea/detail*
   ② —*supporting idea/detail*

➢ **Step 2: Write your response.**
Start by writing a topic sentence that clearly states your main idea. If you're presenting more than one main idea, you will write a topic sentence for each one. The box on page 29 contains guidelines for writing topic sentences for open-ended questions.

Most of the time, you can easily convert an open-ended question into a topic sentence. Study the examples below, based on an open-ended item you saw earlier (page 24). Notice how each topic sentence uses many of the same words that appear in the corresponding question.

OPEN-ENDED ITEM:

David Scott promises that "sooner or later I will succeed, no matter what anyone thinks."

- Identify those qualities that are likely to enable David Scott to achieve his goal.
- Explain what ONE quality you think will prove most important in Scott's struggle to succeed.

SAMPLE TOPIC SENTENCES:

David Scott possesses several qualities that are likely to enable him to achieve his goal.

The one quality that I think will prove most important in Scott's struggle to succeed is. . .

Develop each of your main ideas (topic sentences) with the supporting information that you listed in your plan (Step 1).

As a general rule, each main idea with its supporting information should make up one paragraph. However, if as you're writing you feel that your response would be improved by blending two main ideas into one topic sentence, that's fine. Do whatever you think works most effectively.

> ### Step 3: Revise/edit.
> Reread and evaluate your work. Make sure that you have responded to both questions of the open-ended item clearly and completely. Make whatever changes or additions you feel are needed.
>
> To evaluate your work, you'll find it helpful to ask yourself the questions that appear in the "Scoring Guidelines for Open-Ended Items" on page 25.

> ### Step 4: Proofread.
> Check for errors in grammar, punctuation, capitalization, and spelling.

TOPIC SENTENCES FOR OPEN-ENDED QUESTIONS

<u>Do</u> write a topic sentence that

. . . specifically addresses the question.
. . . clearly expresses your main idea.
. . . leads readers smoothly into the supporting information.

<u>Don't</u> write a topic sentence that

. . . is too general or vague.
. . . is too narrow to be effectively developed.

Compare the following examples:

> Open-ended question: *What is it that Nicole learns from her father?*
>
> Effective topic sentence: *Nicole learns from her father that it's more important to think for herself than to please her friends.*
>
> Too general and vague: *Nicole learns about thinking for herself.*
>
> Too narrow to be a topic sentence: *Nicole learns she was wrong.*

Activity F: Planning a Response

Review "Television Addiction" (pages 9–10) and the "Thinking It Through" on pages 20–22. Also review the notes you took for *Activity B* (page 17). Then, on another sheet of paper, plan a response for the first open-ended item on page 11, shown again below:

11. In paragraph 5, the author states that "a serious addiction is distinguished from a harmless pursuit of pleasure by its distinctly destructive elements."

- What "destructive elements" does the author associate with television viewing?
- How might a TV addict's life change if his/her addiction ended?

Use information from the selection to support your response.

Follow the guidelines above for *Step 1: Plan a Response*.

Activity G: Comparing Plans

Peer feedback. Work with a partner. Compare the plans you made for *Activity F*. Evaluate each other's work, making constructive and specific suggestions. Here are some questions to discuss:

- How are your plans alike?
- How are your plans different?
- What are the strengths of each plan?
- How can each plan be improved?

 Budget Your Time!

The person who administers your test will tell you how much time you have to complete each part of the exam. He or she will also help you keep track of time during the exam.

Be sure to allow yourself enough time to answer the multiple-choice questions and to write a response to the open-ended questions.

Looking at a Sample Plan

Let's see how one student planned a response for the first open-ended item about "Television Addiction." Study the sample plan below. Later in this chapter, you'll see the actual response based on this plan.

After you've examined the sample plan, go on to *Activity H*.

STUDENT'S PLAN FOR OPEN-ENDED ITEM

Note: For example purposes, this plan may be more detailed than yours would need to be. *Your plan needs to be just detailed enough for you to know what you're going to write.*

Destructive elements of TV viewing
  ① —*TV takes place of "activities that lead to growth or development or sense of accomplishment" (P9)*
  ② —*distorts sense of time (P10)*
  ③ —*distorts sense of reality (P10)*
  ④ —*weakens relationships: reduces/eliminates opportunities for interaction (P10)*

How TV addict's life might change if addiction ended
  ① —*more in control of time*
  ② —*more actively involved in life*
  ③ —*more productive*
  ④ —*more social*
  ⑤ —*more likely to deal with problems if not deferring them through TV (P7)*

Activity H: Examining a Plan

Answer the following questions about the student's plan.

1. What are the strengths of the plan?

_____
_____
_____
_____
_____

2. On what two main ideas did the student base the organization?

_____
_____
_____
_____
_____

3. Explain how the supporting information develops the main ideas.

_____
_____
_____
_____
_____

4. How did answering the multiple-choice questions help the student make the plan?

_____

_____

_____

_____

_____

5. How will including the paragraph numbers be useful?

_____

_____

_____

_____

_____

Activity I: Comparing Plans

Compare the sample plan above with the plan you made for *Activity F* (page 29). Then answer the following questions. Be specific in your answers.

1. How do the two plans differ?

_____

_____

_____

2. In what ways do you think your plan may be better than the sample plan?

_____

_____

_____

3. In what ways may the sample plan be stronger than yours?

_____

_____

_____

Writing a Response Based on a Plan

The time you devote to planning your response is well spent. You'll find that working from a clear outline makes the actual writing go smoothly.

Remember that you can always change your plan as you're writing. If you think of a better way to organize ideas, or you want to add (or omit) supporting information, go ahead. Your plan is there to guide you, but you may have new insights as you go along.

Let's see how the student used the plan on page 31 to write a response. First, review the student's plan. Then read the actual response, below.

STUDENT'S RESPONSE TO OPEN-ENDED ITEM

The author associates several "destructive elements" with television viewing. First, for television addicts, TV takes the place of more productive activities. Instead of spending time doing something that leads to self-improvement or accomplishment, an addict passively watches TV. Second, TV's hypnotic power distorts both the addict's sense of time and his or her sense of reality. Third, by limiting chances for social interaction, TV weakens an addict's relationships with other people.

A TV addict's life would be much improved if his or her addiction ended. Free of TV's grip, addicts would be more in control of their time. They could be more actively involved in life's activities and become more productive. They would also have more free time to spend socially with others. In addition, people are more likely to deal with their problems if they are not escaping them by watching TV.

The student's plan guided the content and structure of the response. Each paragraph is based on a main idea, stated in a topic sentence. The student developed the two main ideas with supporting information from the selection.

Note also the following points:

- The student did *not* simply copy supporting information from the selection. Instead, the student *paraphrased* ideas and details—restated them in different words—and clarified or expanded them when appropriate.
- The student adjusted the plan as needed. For example, in the outline, *distorts sense of time* and *distorts sense of reality* were separate supporting details. In the response, the student combined the two.
- The student used transitional words such as *first, second,* and *in addition* to connect ideas and guide the reader. You'll learn more about transitional words and phrases in Chapter 4.

 Making the Most of the Selection

As you write your response, refer back to the selection for clarification and additional information whenever you need to. Your notes and your plan will guide you, but use the selection as your *complete* source of information.

Activity J: Evaluating a Response

Answer the following questions about the student's response.

1. Review the box *TOPIC SENTENCES FOR OPEN-ENDED QUESTIONS* on page 29. How well do the student's topic sentences follow the guidelines? Explain your answer.

    First topic sentence:

    _____

    _____

    _____

    _____

    _____

    Second topic sentence:

    _____

    _____

    _____

    _____

    _____

2. The following questions are based on the "Scoring Guidelines for Open-Ended Items" (page 25). Use the questions to evaluate the student's response. For each question, rate the response on a scale of 1 to 4, with 4 being the highest possible score and 1 being the lowest.

    *   Did the student understand the selection?

        SCORE: _____
    *   Did the student understand the questions and the writing task?

        SCORE: _____
    *   How clearly and effectively did the student answer the questions?

        SCORE: _____
    *   How much insight into the selection and the questions did the student's answer show?

        SCORE: _____
    *   Did the student adequately support his/her answer with ideas and details from the selection?

        SCORE: _____

USING QUOTATION MARKS

When you write a response, you may want to quote portions of a selection to support your ideas. Follow these guidelines to use quotation marks correctly.

Use quotation marks to set off a* direct *quotation—the exact words of a writer or speaker.

> Direct quotation: *The author writes that "the governor simply doesn't understand the needs of average citizens."*

Do* not *use quotation marks with an* indirect *quotation—a restatement, or paraphrase, of a writer's or speaker's words.

> Indirect quotation: *The author says that the governor just doesn't understand the people.*

Always place commas and periods that come at the end of a quotation* inside *the quotation marks.

> *"Plan for tomorrow," the author writes. The author urges everyone to "plan for tomorrow."*

When you want to leave out words from a quotation, use an ellipsis (. . .) to show that words are omitted.

> Complete text: *Lisa is a hard worker, a girl who takes her studies seriously.*

> Quotation: *The author writes that "Lisa . . . takes her studies seriously."*

Use quotation marks to set off titles of* short *works, such as poems, articles, essays, and stories.

> Short works: "Caged Bird" (poem), "Buying a Home Computer" (article), "The Necklace" (story)

For* long *works, such as books, plays, magazines, and newspapers, use underlining.

> Long works: <u>Lord of the Flies</u> (book), <u>Hamlet</u> (play), <u>Newsweek</u> (magazine), <u>The Star-Ledger</u> (newspaper)

REVIEW

Here's a brief summary of the strategies you've learned in Chapter 2. To review any of these strategies in detail, refer to the pages shown.

Reading actively (pages 13–14):
→ Get information from the introduction.
→ Think about the selection title.
→ Skim the questions before you read.
→ Read carefully and thoughtfully.
→ Pay attention to text features and visual aids.
→ Reread and think about difficult parts.
→ Consider the author's use of literary elements and techniques.
→ Take notes.

Taking notes (pages 14–15):
→ Use a simplified outline form.
→ Keep your notes short, simple, and clear.
→ Include paragraph numbers for reference.
→ Note details that relate to questions you'll have to answer.
→ Use shortcuts.
→ Highlight notes that are especially important.

Answering the multiple-choice questions (pages 18–19):
→ Make sure that you understand the *question* before you consider the answer choices.
→ Identify key words in questions.
→ Read and compare *all* the choices. Then choose the best and most complete answer.
→ Refer to the reading selection, and to your notes, as often as you need to.
→ Use context to help you.
→ Narrow your search.
→ Don't get stuck on a difficult question.
→ Be sure to answer every question.

Answering the open-ended questions (pages 26–29):
→ Make sure that you understand the question.
→ Identify key words in questions.
→ Use context to help you.
→ Refer to the reading selection, and to your notes, as often as you need to.
→ Follow these four steps: (1) make a plan; (2) write your response; (3) revise/edit; (4) proofread.

PRACTICE

The activities that follow will give you a chance to practice the strategies that you learned in this chapter. You'll have further opportunities to apply these strategies throughout this book.

Practice Activity 1

Plan and write a response for the *second* open-ended item on page 11, shown again below:

12. The author compares television viewing to drug and alcohol use.

   • In what ways does the author see the two as similar?
   • What aspect of television viewing do you think the author considers most harmful?

Use information from the selection to support your response.

Before beginning, you may want to review "Television Addiction" (pages 9–10), the "Thinking It Through " on pages 20–22, and the notes you took for *Activity B* (page 17).

Remember to follow the four steps for developing a response:

   Step 1:   Make a plan.
   Step 2:   Write your response.
   Step 3:   Revise/edit.
   Step 4:   Proofread.

_____
_____
_____
_____
_____
_____
_____
_____
_____
_____
_____
_____
_____
_____
_____

_____

_____

_____

_____

_____

_____

_____

_____

_____

Practice Activity 2

A. **Peer feedback**. Work with a partner. Exchange the responses you wrote for *Practice Activity 1*, and evaluate each other's work on the basis of the questions shown below. Make constructive and specific suggestions to help your partner improve his/her skills.

- Did the student understand the selection?
- Did the student understand the questions and the writing task?
- How clearly and effectively did the student answer the questions?
- How much insight into the selection and the questions did the student's answer show?
- Did the student adequately support his/her answer with ideas and details from the selection?

B. Use your partner's comments to help you revise your response. Make whatever changes you think will improve your work.

Practice Activity 3

For this activity, you'll apply the strategies you've learned to *narrative* text. Read the selection and answer the questions that follow.

Sometimes well-intentioned efforts do not lead to desired results. The following story, set in a Nigerian village, explores this idea through the experience of a young teacher.

Dead Men's Path
by Chinua Achebe

Michael Obi's hopes were fulfilled much earlier than he expected. He was appointed headmaster of Ndume Central School in January 1949. It had always been an unprogressive school, so the Mission authorities decided to send a young and energetic man to run it. Obi accepted this responsibility with enthusiasm. He had many wonderful ideas and this was an opportunity to put them into practice. He had had sound secondary school education which designated him a "pivotal teacher" in the official records and set him apart from the other headmasters in the mission field. He was outspoken in his condemnation of the narrow views of these older and often less-educated ones.

"We shall make a good job of it, shan't we?" he asked his young wife when they first heard the joyful news of his promotion.

"We shall do our best," she replied. "We shall have such beautiful gardens and everything will be just *modern* and delightful . . ." In their two years of married life she had become completely infected by his passion for "modern methods" and his denigration of "these old and superannuated people in the teaching field who would be better employed as traders in the Onitsha market." She began to see herself already as the admired wife of the young headmaster, the queen of the school.

The wives of the other teachers would envy her position. She would set the fashion in everything . . . Then, suddenly, it occurred to her that there might not be other wives. Wavering between hope and fear, she asked her husband, looking anxiously at him.

"All our colleagues are young and unmarried," he said with enthusiasm which for once she did not share. "Which is a good thing," he continued.

"Why?"

"Why? They will give all their time and energy to the school."

Nancy was downcast. For a few minutes she became skeptical about the new school; but it was only for a few minutes. Her little personal misfortune could not blind her to her husband's happy prospects. She looked at him as he sat folded up in a chair. He was stoop-shouldered and looked frail. But he sometimes surprised people with sudden bursts of physical energy. In his present posture, however, all his bodily strength seemed to have retired behind his deep-set eyes, giving them an extraordinary power of penetration. He was only twenty-six, but looked thirty or more. On the whole, he was not unhandsome.

"A penny for your thoughts, Mike," said Nancy after a while, imitating the woman's magazine she read.

"I was thinking what a grand opportunity we've got at last to show these people how a school should be run."

Ndume School was backward in every sense of the word. Mr. Obi put his whole life into the work, and his wife hers too. He had two aims. A high standard of teaching was insisted upon, and the school compound was to be turned into a place of beauty. Nancy's dream-gardens came to life with the coming of the rains, and blossomed. Beautiful hibiscus and allamanda hedges in brilliant red and yellow marked out the carefully tended school compound from the rank neighbourhood bushes.

12   One evening as Obi was admiring his work he was <u>scandalized</u> to see an old woman from the village hobble right

across the compound, through a marigold flower-bed and the hedges. On going up there he found faint signs of an almost disused path from the village across the school compound to the bush on the other side.

"It amazes me," said Obi to one of his teachers who had been three years in the school, "that you people allowed the villagers to make use of this footpath. It is simply incredible." He shook his head.

"The path," said the teacher apologetically, "appears to be very important to them. Although it is hardly used, it connects the village shrine with their place of burial."

"And what has that got to do with the school?" asked the headmaster.

"Well, I don't know," replied the other with a shrug of the shoulders. "But I remember there was a big row some time ago when we attempted to close it."

"That was some time ago. But it will not be used now," said Obi as he walked away. "What will the Government Education Officer think of this when he comes to inspect the school next week? The villagers might, for all I know, decide to use the schoolroom for a pagan ritual during the inspection."

Heavy sticks were planted closely across the path at the   **18** two places where it entered and left the school premises. These were further strengthened with barbed wire.

Three days later the village priest of *Ani* called on the headmaster. He was an old man and walked with a slight stoop. He carried a stout walking-stick which he usually tapped on the floor, by way of emphasis, each time he made a new point in his argument.

"I have heard," he said after the usual exchange of cordialities, "that our ancestral footpath has recently been closed . . . "

"Yes," replied Mr. Obi. "We cannot allow people to make a highway of our school compound."

"Look here, my son," said the priest bringing down his walking-stick, "this path was here before you were born and before your father was born. The whole life of this village depends on it. Our dead relatives depart by it and our ancestors visit us by it. But most important, it is the path of children coming in to be born . . . "

Mr. Obi listened with a satisfied smile on his face.

"The whole purpose of our school," he said finally, "is to <u>eradicate</u> just such beliefs as that. Dead men do not re-   **24** quire footpaths. The whole idea is just fantastic. Our duty is to teach your children to laugh at such ideas."

"What you say may be true," replied the priest, "but we follow the practices of our fathers. If you re-open the path we shall have nothing to quarrel about. What I always say is: let the hawk perch and let the eagle perch." He rose to go.

"I am sorry," said the young headmaster. "But the school compound cannot be a thoroughfare. It is against our regulations. I would suggest your constructing another path, skirting our premises. We can even get our boys to help in building it. I don't suppose the ancestors will find the little detour too burdensome."

"I have no more words to say," said the old priest, already outside.

Two days later a young woman in the village died in childbed. A diviner was immediately consulted and he prescribed heavy sacrifices to <u>propitiate</u> ancestors insulted by the fence.

28

Obi woke up the next morning among the ruins of his work. The beautiful hedges were torn up not just near the path but right round the school, the flowers trampled to death and one of the school buildings pulled down . . . That day, the white Supervisor came to inspect the school and wrote a nasty report on the state of the premises but more seriously about the "tribal-war situation developing between the school and the village, arising in part from the misguided zeal of the new headmaster."

1. In paragraph 12, the author writes that Mr. Obi "was **scandalized** to see an old woman from the village hobble right across the compound. . . ." In this context, **scandalized** means

   A. amused.
   B. shocked.
   C. encouraged.
   D. scared.

2. What was the purpose of the heavy sticks and the barbed wire (paragraph 18)?

   A. to keep out the villagers' ancestors
   B. to protect the village shrine
   C. to prevent villagers from crossing school grounds
   D. to guide villagers safely along the path

3. Mr. Obi regarded the villagers' beliefs with

   A. contempt.
   B. fear.
   C. curiosity.
   D. respect.

4. When a young woman of the village died giving birth, the villagers

   A. thought the village priest was at fault.
   B. believed her death was a coincidence.
   C. held the Supervisor responsible.
   D. blamed the closing of the path.

5. In paragraph 28, the author refers to "sacrifices needed to **propitiate** ancestors insulted by the fence." The word **propitiate** means

   A. entertain.
   B. reward.
   C. calm.
   D. deceive.

6. Mr. Obi wants to impress the Supervisor with his actions, but his efforts have the opposite result. This is an example of

   A. satire.
   B. symbolism.
   C. elaboration.
   D. irony.

7. Which of the following quotations best supports the major theme of the story?

   A. "He was stoop-shouldered and looked frail. But he sometimes surprised people with sudden bursts of physical energy."
   B. "This path was here before you were born and before your father was born. The whole life of this village depends on it."
   C. "Nancy's dream-gardens came to life with the coming of the rains, and blossomed."
   D. "Michael Obi's hopes were fulfilled much earlier than he expected."

8. A key conflict in this story is the clash between

    A. good and evil.
    B. truth and falsehood.
    C. old and new.
    D. right and wrong.

9. The word **eradicate** as Mr. Obi uses it in paragraph 24 means

    A. eliminate.
    B. encourage.
    C. make public.
    D. establish.

10. Based on his words and actions, Mr. Obi can best be described as

    A. unsure.
    B. arrogant.
    C. considerate.
    D. patient.

OPEN-ENDED ITEM

11. There is a biblical saying that "pride goeth before destruction, and an haughty spirit before a fall."

    • How do Mr. Obi's "pride" and "haughty spirit" lead to the Supervisor's negative report about the school?
    • How might Mr. Obi's experience affect his approach to his work in the future?

    Use information from the story to support your response.

    _____

    _____

    _____

    _____

    _____

    _____

    _____

_____

_____

_____

_____

_____

_____

_____

_____

_____

USING YOUR READING AND THINKING SKILLS

The Language Arts HSPA asks you to analyze and interpret the ideas and information presented in two reading selections. To do this, you'll have to apply your language arts reading and thinking skills. This chapter will zero in on many of the skills you'll need.

Bear in mind that you'll usually apply more than one skill at a time. That's because language arts skills are *interconnected*. For example, to understand an author's purpose, you may have to make inferences and draw conclusions about the author's ideas.

Individual skills are viewed separately in this chapter only as a way of highlighting specific elements. In use, *the skills work together*.

Note, too, that you can apply the same basic skills and strategies to narrative, persuasive, and informational text. Also, you'll put these skills to use to answer multiple-choice *and* open-ended questions.

Finally, remember that the same language arts skills that you use for the HSPA will also help you with *all* the reading you do, both in and out of school.

This chapter will help you do your best on the HSPA tasks highlighted below.

☑ HSPA READING AND WRITING TASKS

	Part 1:	Write an extended response about a picture.
✔	**Part 2:**	Read a persuasive selection and answer multiple-choice and open-ended questions.
	Part 3:	Revise and edit a given student essay.
✔	**Part 4:**	Read a narrative selection and answer multiple-choice and open-ended questions.
	Part 5:	Write a persuasive essay or letter.

3.1 IDENTIFYING IMPORTANT IDEAS AND INFORMATION

THE BASICS

Every selection has a point. That point might be to show the horrors of war, to propose the construction of a new highway, or to describe a significant childhood event.

Authors get their point across in various ways. Compare the examples below.

MAKING A POINT

Selection	Central Idea	How the Author Makes the Point
essay	High school students have to take too many tests.	Describes the numerous tests students must take; includes statistics showing how much time students spend taking tests
short story	To reach one's goal, a person must keep trying.	Main character overcomes numerous obstacles to achieve her goal
article	Medical breakthroughs are allowing people to live longer, healthier lives.	Describes some of the most significant advances in medicine

One of your primary goals as a reader is to figure out what the point of a selection is. To do this, you need to understand the ideas and details that the author presents and how they are all related.

Central Idea

The *central idea* is the principal point of a selection, the main focus or underlying meaning. The central idea is also sometimes called the *theme*, *thesis*, or *controlling idea*.

The central idea of a selection may be directly stated or it may be implied. In persuasive and informational text, authors usually state their central idea directly. In narrative text, authors more commonly *imply* their point through events and characters.

Narrative? Persuasive? Other?

Many selections that you'll read in school and on your own will not fit neatly into one category. For example, "narrative" text may convey information or describe a true personal experience. "Informational" text may tell an interesting story or subtly try to persuade readers to accept the author's point of view.

Main Ideas and Supporting Information

The paragraphs that make up a selection work together to develop the central idea. The *main idea* of a paragraph is the idea that holds the paragraph together. It's what the whole paragraph is about. Like the central idea, main ideas may be directly stated or implied.

If the main idea of a paragraph is directly stated, it's often expressed in a *topic sentence*. However, not every paragraph has a topic sentence. Furthermore, while topic sentences are common in nonfiction selections, they appear only occasionally in fiction.

Authors develop and support their ideas with *supporting information*, such as facts, details, examples, and reasons. The supporting information in a paragraph tells more about the main idea. Study the following diagram.

PARTS OF A WHOLE

Understanding the structure of a selection will help you to understand what the author is trying to say. For example, in a typical persuasive or informational selection, main ideas work together to support the central idea.

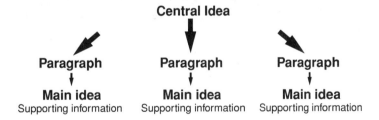

Activity A: Examining the Structure of an Article

Choose a persuasive or informational article or essay from a magazine or newspaper. Answer the following questions about the selection.

1. What is the central idea of the selection?

   _____

   _____

2. Explain how the paragraphs of the selection work together to support and develop the central idea.

   _____

   _____

   _____

3. What kinds of supporting information does the writer include? Give specific examples.

   _____

   _____

   _____

   _____

STRATEGIES

Use the following strategies to identify the central idea, main ideas, and supporting information in the HSPA selections. Remember that each selection is unique. You have to adapt the strategies to individual selections.

Identifying the Central Idea of a Selection

To identify the central idea of *persuasive* or *informational* text:

➤ **Think about the title and the introduction.**
   The title often suggests what the selection is about. The introduction (if there is one) provides information about the selection and sometimes about the author's purpose for writing.

➤ **Think about the main ideas and supporting information.**
   Ask yourself how the main ideas are connected and what underlying idea they all relate to. Consider what supporting information the author has chosen to include, and why.

   Watch for a pattern. For example, if an author describes many examples of needless violence in TV shows, what might the author be saying about the quality of television?

➤ **Think about organization and structure.**
   Be aware of how the author has organized the content. Three common methods of organization are described in the box on page 51.

➤ **Consider the selection as a whole.**
   Ask yourself: *What's the point of this selection? Why did the author write it?* The answers to these questions will point you toward the central idea.

➤ **Pay special attention to the beginning and end.**
   The opening and closing paragraphs of a selection often summarize or repeat new central idea.

You can use these same strategies to identify the central idea of narrative text, such as a short story. However, because authors of narrative text are more likely to *imply* their ideas, you'll have to rely more on your ability to make inferences.

You'll learn more about making inferences in section 3.2, "Making Inferences and Drawing Conclusions." For now, here are some strategies to help you identify the central idea of *narrative* text:

> ➤ **Consider and compare characters.**
> Think about their words, thoughts, and actions. Which characters does the author show in a positive light? Which are shown in a negative light? Why?

> ➤ **Think about the story's events and their outcome.**
> What conflict is involved in the plot? How is it resolved? What happens as a result of characters' actions? What message may the author be sending? For example, are deceitful characters punished for their deceit?

> ➤ **Think about the author's techniques.**
> What literary devices does the author use to communicate ideas? For example, does the author use symbolism to suggest a deeper level of meaning? You'll read more about literary elements and techniques in section 3.5, "Examining Elements of Fiction and Nonfiction."

 The Concepts Behind the Words

Some HSPA questions use terms such as *central idea, theme,* and *main idea.* However, many questions that *don't* use such terms still relate directly or indirectly to the concepts behind them. In other words, you'll need to recognize central idea, main ideas, and supporting information even when questions don't say so in those exact words.

Think about these examples:

> *What does the author learn from her experience?*
> (central idea)
>
> *Why does the general refuse to surrender?*
> (main idea)
>
> *Why does Aliya rush home after the party?*
> (supporting information)

Activity B: Identifying Central Ideas

Circle the correct answers.

1. In an essay about the justice system outside the United States, the author describes the following:

   - In one foreign country, the prime minister hires and fires all judges, and they answer only to the prime minister.
   - In another country, people who oppose the government are arrested for expressing their views.
   - In a third country, a woman who stole a loaf of bread was sentenced to five years in prison, while the president's brother received a three-month sentence for a hit-and-run accident in which two people were killed.

   Which of the following is the most likely central idea of the essay?

   A. Only wealthy people receive justice.
   B. The notion of "justice" in some countries is a joke.
   C. Crime never pays.
   D. Politicians cannot be trusted.

2. In a short story, an understudy deliberately causes an accident in which the star of the show breaks his leg. The understudy takes over the role, but he gets awful reviews from every newspaper and magazine.

   Which of the following is the most likely central idea of the story?

   A. The end justifies the means.
   B. Life is seldom fair.
   C. Hard work always pays off in the end.
   D. People usually get what they deserve.

Identifying Main Ideas

➤ **Look for a topic sentence.**
   The topic sentence—if the paragraph has one—states the main idea. It's often the first sentence in a paragraph, but it may also appear in the middle of a paragraph or at the end.

➤ **Consider the overall paragraph.**
   Ask yourself what idea underlies the whole paragraph. If the main idea is implied rather than stated, figure it out by examining the supporting information. What do the supporting facts, details, and examples have in common? How do they all fit together? Try to summarize the point of the paragraph in your own words.

➤ **Consider how the part fits into the whole.**
Together, the paragraphs of a selection develop a central idea. You can use this fact to help you figure out what a paragraph is about. For example, if the first few paragraphs of a selection describe the benefits of owning a pet, it's likely that the following paragraphs will continue to develop that theme.

➤ **Watch for words that signal main ideas.**
Certain phrases call attention to important ideas. Here are some examples:

the main reason that　　　*the chief result*
the single most important　*above all*
the greatest problem　　　*most of all*

Identifying Supporting Information

➤ **Use the main idea as your guide.**
Much as supporting information can guide you toward main ideas, so can main ideas point you toward important supporting information. For example, if a paragraph expresses the main idea in a topic sentence, look for specific information that supports or develops that idea.

➤ **Ask yourself the "5 W's + H."**
When journalists gather information, they try to answer six questions. These questions are sometimes referred to as the "5 W's + H":

Who?
　What?
　　Where?
　　　When?
　　　　Why?
　　　　　How?

You can ask yourself these same questions to identify supporting information. Of course, not every paragraph (or even every selection) will contain the answers to all six questions. However, the questions you *can* answer will help you spot important details.

Activity C: Using the "5 W's + H"

Choose a persuasive or informational article or essay (not the same one you used for *Activity A*). Ask yourself the "5 W's + H" to identify important supporting information. Summarize your answers below.

Who?

_____

_____

_____

_____

What?

_____

_____

_____

_____

Where?

_____

_____

_____

_____

When?

_____

_____

_____

_____

Why?

_____

_____

_____

_____

How?

_____

_____

_____

_____

METHODS OF ORGANIZATION

Writers organize their content in many different ways. Three of the most common methods of organization are shown below. Writers may use these methods to organize:

the paragraphs that make up a selection
or
the ideas and information *within* a paragraph.

Order of increasing *importance/interest*
Ideas and supporting information are arranged in order from the least important/interesting to the most important/ interesting. Writers often use this approach when they want to build to a conclusion.

third most important idea →
    second most important idea →
        most important idea of all

Order of decreasing *importance/interest*
Ideas and supporting information are arranged in order from the most important/interesting to the least important/interesting. Writers may use this approach when they want to lead off with a strong point and then add additional points.

most important idea →
    second most important idea →
        third most important idea

Chronological (time) order
Facts, details, or events are presented in time order, usually moving forward in time. Writers may use this form of organization to describe a sequence of events or to explain a cause-and-effect relationship.

what happened first →
    what happened next →
        what happened after that

Note that writers sometimes combine methods. Or, they may use different methods in different paragraphs. There are no absolute rules. Note, too, that you may use these same methods of organization when *you* write.

You can read more about how writers organize and develop their content in "Patterns of Development," on pages 70–72.

/// **APPLYING YOUR KNOWLEDGE**

1. Read the selection and answer the questions. Use the strategies that you learned in this chapter *and* in Chapter 2. (For a summary of Chapter 2 strategies, turn to "Review" on page 36.)

2. After you've finished, read "Thinking It Through" to see how one student answered the questions.

Deep in the rain forest, dedicated scientists and trackers are risking their lives to save this rare primate from extinction.

Last Stand of the Mountain Gorilla
by Paul Raffaelle

1 For more than five hours our expedition has battled up the rugged rainforest slopes of a volcano in Rwanda, central Africa. We are tracking a group of nomadic[1] mountain gorillas, the rarest and largest of the great apes. As we rise to 12,000 feet, my lungs are ready to burst, but our three trackers relentlessly lead on. Swinging machetes, they carve a narrow path through the vines and bamboo.

2 At midafternoon our path is abruptly blocked by a giant silverback, a six-foot, 400-pound male gorilla perched on a slope above us. He is swathed in jet-black hair, except for his back, which glistens silvery white. His brawny arms are several times thicker than a weightlifter's, and his crested head is bigger than a bull's.

3 English veterinarian Jonathan Sleeman quickly pulls me to the ground and imitates a submissive pose used by lower-ranking gorillas. "His name is Kwakane, and he's got a grudge against me," Sleeman whispers.

4 Suddenly the gorilla roars a ferocious battle cry. We cannot retreat, for to do so would provoke a charge. Sleeman nervously plucks a vine leaf and grips it with his teeth. I join him in this gesture of peace.

5 Kwakane is not persuaded. He stands and pounds his great chest. The thock, thock, thock turns my heart to water. Then without warning he charges straight at us on all fours, his massive hands and feet slamming against the ground.

6 After thriving for hundreds of thousands of years, mountain gorillas are now endangered. A surging tide of humans has pushed these apes into just two areas of rain forest in central Africa. Only 600 mountain gorillas are left, about half living on the slopes of the Virungas, a curve of volcanoes straddling the border between Rwanda, Zaire, and Uganda.

7 "Their gene pool is so limited that even the loss of a few puts the species at peril," says Sleeman, field director of the Mountain Gorilla Veterinary Center in Rwanda. "We are fighting desperately to save them. It is a courageous battle, one of the most inspiring conservation efforts of our time."

8 **Gentle Giants.** Local inhabitants have always feared the gorillas. In 1861, British explorer John Speke was warned that the volcano slopes were inhabited by manlike monsters. The mountain gorillas were unknown to Western scientists until 1902, when a German explorer shot two. Over the next 25 years hunters killed or captured more than 50 of the rare primates. By the 1960s, with the human populations of Rwanda and Zaire exploding, much of the gorillas' highland habitat had been taken, leaving 450 of the apes squeezed into the Virungas. By 1981, there were just 254 left.

9 Their unlikely savior was American primatologist[2] Dian Fossey, author of *Gorillas in the Mist*. Setting up the research center in Rwanda in 1967, Fossey trained a crew of trackers to monitor the gorillas and lead her to them

[1]Moving from place to place with no fixed home.

[2]Scientist who studies apes, monkeys, or humans.

each day. She soon alerted the world to their threatened extinction.

Among her recruits was Fidele Nshogoza. Over a shared pot of *pombe*—banana beer—Nshogoza, now 47, told me of his first encounter with the gorillas. He came across **10** more than a dozen sprawled in an alpine meadow, looking just like a family on a picnic. Nshogoza watched as the brawny patriarch lay on his belly, resting his chin on blockbuster arms. *"Le grand chef,"* Nshogoza whispered in awe. "The chieftain."

Gathered about the leader were his six wives, typically less than half his size. An imp-faced youngster clambered onto the silverback's shoulders, pulling his hair in fun. **11** The father let the infant yank away. *The silverback has the power of several men,* Nshogoza thought, *but is so gentle with his family.* The great ape was not the monster of native legend.

Over the years, Fossey monitored three groups of more than 50 gorillas. But in December 1985 she was hacked **12** to death, many believe by poachers angry at her efforts to force them from their hunting grounds. Nshogoza was numb with shock, but dedicated himself to continuing Fossey's work.

Then, in April 1994, Rwanda erupted in brutal warfare between the Hutus and Tutsis. As the genocide unfolded, Nshogoza, a Hutu, was forced to join his family in exile **13** in neighboring Zaire. From there, he would gaze up at the misty blue volcano peaks and worry about the gorillas, unprotected amid the carnage.

Finally, he crossed back into Rwanda, braving the machete-armed militias, and roamed the Virungas. He was **14** relieved to find all the gorillas safe.

Common Ancestor. Today the threat of renewed bloodshed still looms. Many people nonetheless carry on their courageous work to save the gorillas. One afternoon I am with Justin Rurangirwa-Nyampeta, conservator of Parc National des Volcans on the Rwanda side of the Virungas. **15** He points to the many mud-hut villages that lap against the volcanoes' foothills. "We have to send out daily patrols to prevent villagers from going into the forest for firewood or to forage for their cattle," he says. "The destruction threatens the gorillas' habitat."

Rurangirwa-Nyampeta is working to shield the gorillas by reforesting the park's border. "Many wonder why we **16** devote so much attention to the gorillas," he says. "It is because they are so precious they belong to the world."

1. What is the central idea of this article?

    A. Mountain gorillas threaten the lives of nearby human beings.
    B. Warfare between Hutus and Tutsis has caused the death of many mountain gorillas.
    C. Mountain gorillas are finally out of danger.
    D. Dedicated individuals are trying to save the mountain gorilla from extinction.

2. According to the article, mountain gorillas are losing their natural habitat to

    A. other animals.
    B. humans.
    C. forces of nature.
    D. volcanoes.

3. According to the article (paragraph 11), mountain gorillas

    A. are far more dangerous than people realize.
    B. exist only in legend.
    C. make poor caregivers to their young.
    D. are powerful, yet gentle with their families.

4. Why does the author refer to Dian Fossey as the mountain gorillas' "savior"?

    A. She first made the world aware that the gorillas were endangered.
    B. She ended the war between Hutus and Tutsis.
    C. She relocated the gorillas to a safer part of Africa.
    D. She taught the gorillas how to survive in the wild.

Thinking It Through

1. What is the central idea of this article?

   A. Mountain gorillas threaten the lives of nearby human beings.
   B. Warfare between Hutus and Tutsis has caused the death of many mountain gorillas.
   C. Mountain gorillas are finally out of danger.
   D. Dedicated individuals are trying to save the mountain gorilla from extinction.

   The title of the article seems to suggest choice D as the central idea. After considering all the choices, I know that answer is correct. It's the only answer that is supported and developed by the article as a whole.

2. According to the article, mountain gorillas are losing their natural habitat to

   A. other animals.
   B. humans.
   C. forces of nature.
   D. volcanoes.

   Paragraphs 6, 8, and 15 all refer to the idea of humans taking away the gorillas' habitat. The correct answer is B.

3. According to paragraph 11 of the article, mountain gorillas

   A. are far more dangerous than people realize.
   B. exist only in legend.
   C. make poor caregivers to their young.
   D. are powerful, yet gentle with their families.

   The main idea of paragraph 11 is Nshogoza's thought that the gorilla "has the power of several men . . . but is so gentle with his family." Choice B is clearly wrong, and choice C is not supported by the text. Choice A may be true, but it's not an idea developed in paragraph 11. Choice D is the correct answer.

4. Why does the author refer to Dian Fossey as the mountain gorillas' "savior" (paragraph 9)?

   A. She first made the world aware that the gorillas were endangered.
   B. She ended the war between Hutus and Tutsis.
   C. She relocated the gorillas to a safer part of Africa.
   D. She taught the gorillas how to survive in the wild.

   The last sentence of paragraph 9 helps me decide that choice A is the correct answer. Also, none of the other answers is supported by the text.

Focus on the Selection Itself

Some HSPA selections may deal with subjects that you know something about. Don't be distracted. Base your answers on the ideas and information in the selection itself.

Similarly, don't let your knowledge or opinions tempt you to choose an incorrect answer. For example, suppose that one possible answer to a multiple-choice question is a statement that you agree with. Choose that answer only if it is supported by the selection itself.

REVIEW

Here's a brief summary of what you've learned in section 3.1. To review any of these points in detail, turn to the pages shown.

The basics (pages 44–46):

→ The *central idea* is the principal point of a selection, the main focus or underlying meaning. The central idea is also sometimes called the *theme, thesis,* or *controlling idea.*

→ The *main idea* of a paragraph is the idea that holds the paragraph together. It's what the whole paragraph is about.

→ Authors develop main ideas with *supporting information,* such as facts, details, examples, and reasons.

Identifying the central idea (pages 46–48):
(*any* selection)

→ Think about the title and the introduction.

→ Think about the main ideas and supporting information.

→ Think about organization and structure.

→ Consider the selection as a whole.

→ Pay special attention to the beginning and end.

→ Consider and compare characters.

→ Think about the story's events and their outcome.

→ Think about the author's techniques.

Identifying main ideas (pages 48–49):
(*narrative* text)

→ Look for a topic sentence.

→ Consider the overall paragraph.

→ Consider how the part fits into the whole.

→ Watch for words that signal main ideas.

Identifying supporting information (pages 49–50):

→ Use the main idea as your guide.

→ Ask yourself the "5 W's + H": who, what, where, when, why, and how.

PRACTICE

The activities that follow will give you a chance to practice the strategies that you learned in this chapter *and* in Chapter 2. (For a summary of Chapter 2 strategies, turn to "Review" on page 36.

Because HSPA questions call for a combination of skills, some practice questions touch on skills covered in other parts of this book.

Practice Activity 1

Read the selection and answer the questions that follow.

Countless novels and movies have pictured extraterrestrial life—beings from outer space. In this article, the writer discusses the realities of scientists' search for other life in the universe.

The Search for Extraterrestrial Life
by John P. Wiley, Jr.

Somebody must be out there. On all those worlds circling red suns, blue suns, double suns, giant suns, pulsing suns: somewhere somebody is. Modern science stretches our intuition to the breaking point, or turns it upside down and inside out, and yet intuition is not always wrong simply because it is intuition. And intuition tells us that in a universe of billions of galaxies, each with billions of suns, there must be somebody else. If life can arise once, surely it can arise more than once.

2 Life elsewhere can reasonably be expected to be older than ours. The solar system we live in is only about 4.6 billion years old, a half or less than the age of the universe we see. The cosmos is filled with older stars that would have older planets on which life could have arisen much longer ago than on Earth. The possibilities make the mind ache as much as do the distances involved.

3 Imagine ourselves walking around in 986 and speculating on what the next 1,000 years would bring. Could anyone have guessed at how much the human mind would come to understand of biology? It would be another 900 years before we even knew how diseases are transmitted. Would we have happily assented to the idea that the Earth is not the center of the universe, or that there are other galaxies? Today we smile, but can any of us guess what we will know in another 1,000 years? Not to mention 10,000? My intuition fails. Yet if there are other civilizations out there, they may be not ten thousand, but ten million years older than ours. And if such a civilization developed the equivalent of open-heart surgery, laser communication and space flight ten million years ago, what are they doing today?

4 As 1985 ended, scientists were looking back on a quarter century of looking for signs of such advanced civilizations with not a <u>scintilla</u> of evidence that any exist. During 120,000 hours of listening with the most sophisticated radio telescopes in seven different countries, we did not once hear "Breaker, breaker,"[1] strings of numbers, repeating patterns, any signals of any kind that stood out above the cosmic noise. For twenty-five years we have waited by the telephone and no one has called.

Astronomer Michael D. Papagiannis of Boston University recently reviewed the situation in *Nature*, the British science journal. He is president of Commission 51 of the International Astronomical Union: Search for Extraterrestrial Life. His vice presidents are N. S. Kardashev, a Russian, and Frank D. Drake, who in the spring of 1960 first turned a radio telescope to a nearby star to listen for the signals of intelligent life.

6 According to Papagiannis, we have found nothing so far but we are about to launch our most sophisticated effort yet, and by about the year 2000 (let's make it 2001, in honor of Arthur C. Clarke) we will know a lot more about whether advanced civilizations abound in our galaxy. First Papagiannis reviews our most recent efforts, including some avenues that sound like they are straight out of science fiction. I had not realized that some have been searching with optical telescopes for artifacts, including automated probes, left in our solar system by civilizations from elsewhere. They specifically looked at the stable points in the Earth-Moon and Earth-Sun gravitational

[1]"Breaker, breaker": operator's code expression for "breaking into" a radio network—somewhat like "Hello."

systems, to see if we are being watched by a galactic equivalent of the television cameras stores use to keep an eye on us.

Astronomers in the United States and the Soviet Union have looked at stars that are unusually luminous at infrared wavelengths. They are looking for feats of astro-engineering known as Dyson spheres, named for the Princeton physicist who first suggested them. To make a Dyson sphere, you simply dismantle all the planets around your star and reassemble the material in a hollow shell that envelops the star, catching large parts of its radiation (talk about an advanced civilization!). The trapped radiation would be reemitted out the far side of the shell at infrared wavelengths.

7

Papagiannis himself is gearing up for an infrared search closer to home. Using data from the Infrared Astronomy Satellite, he is going to look for large artificial objects—things like space colonies and processing plants mining the raw materials in the asteroid belt—right here in our own solar system.

8

Most of the search, however, goes on with radio telescopes. Some are directed at specific places in the sky: nearby stars similar to the Sun have been a favorite from the first. But radio astronomers also check what Papagiannis calls magic places. The center of the galaxy, where stars are much closer together than they are in our neighborhood, way out in a spiral arm, seems an obvious place for a supercivilization and a pulsed beacon as a master navigational aid and communication channel.

9

Other searches swing across the entire sky. A radio telescope at Ohio State University has been searching much of the accessible sky since 1973, with some funding from NASA but dependent largely on the work of volunteers. Another whole-sky search, funded by the Planetary Society, has been conducted since March 1983 at the Oak Ridge Harvard-Smithsonian Observatory near Boston.

Now NASA is ready with the next generation of radios and signal detectors. Seeing how far we have come in just twenty-five years is exactly the kind of thing that makes me marvel at the thought of where we—or somebody else—will be in another 10,000 years. When Frank Drake first turned the Green Bank radio telescope toward the stars Epsilon Eridani and Tau Ceti that spring, he used a single-channel receiver. The new searches will be made with multichannel spectrum analyzers, intruments that can scan 8.4 million channels at the same time.

The new program is an all-California affair, centered at the NASA Ames Research Center, the Jet Propulsion Laboratory, and Stanford University. Like previous efforts, it will be divided into a targeted search and an overall sky survey.

The targeted search will use large radio telescopes to look at 773 nearby stars of roughly the size and temperature of the Sun, as well as some other stars with unusual spectra.

The sky survey will use smaller radio telescopes, examining something on the order of a million sections of the sky. The whole thing could be done in five years but realistically will take more like ten, Papagiannis estimates. So if we start around 1990, we will finish up just about at the turn of the century.

The search for extraterrestrial life has always been controversial. Scientists have argued that any advanced civilizations would have been here already. Since there are no signs that they have been here or are here, then they do not exist. Enrico Fermi put it simply a long time ago: "Where are they?"

The search is an old story. It is tedious (imagine looking through the computer printouts of 120,000 hours of telescope time). And, as Papagiannis says," . . . we began to realize that none of us can claim to know how civilizations far more advanced than ours are likely to behave and act."

The whole point is that we do not know that there is not a message. Intuition may be wrong, but we don't know for sure that nobody is out there. For the last twenty-five years, instead of just thinking about the question we have been doing something to answer it. We have moved from speculation to experiment. We are about to do a lot more. And wouldn't it be exciting if . . . ?

1. What is the author's principal point in this article?

_____

_____

_____

2. What is the main idea of paragraph 2?

_____

_____

_____

3. What supporting information does the author use to develop the main idea of paragraph 2?

_____

_____

_____

4. What idea does the author develop in paragraphs 9 and 10?

_____

_____

_____

Practice Activity 2

Review the selection "The Search for Extraterrestrial Life." Then answer the multiple-choice and open-ended questions below.

Reminder: Use the strategies that you learned in this chapter *and* in Chapter 2.

1. Which statement BEST expresses the article's central idea?

    A. The search for alien life forms is a waste of time.
    B. Life may exist outside our planet.
    C. Earthlings are probably the most advanced form of life.
    D. Scientists know for sure that other life forms exist.

2. According to the article, one argument against the possibility of an advanced extraterrestrial civilization is that such a civilization

    A. would have ceased to exist long ago.
    B. could not exist in space.
    C. would already have made contact with Earth.
    D. would have needed Earth's help.

3. In paragraph 2, the author explains that Earth's solar system is younger than other solar systems in the universe. This fact BEST supports which of the following statements?

    A. "Somebody must be out there."
    B. "Life elsewhere can reasonably be expected to be older than ours."
    C. "If life can arise once, surely it can arise more than once."
    D. "The search for extraterrestrial life has always been controversial."

4. The word **scintilla** in paragraph 4 means

    A. fragment.
    B. photograph.

    C. data.
    D. large amount.

5. According to the article, the primary means used to search for extraterrestrial life is

    A. the Dyson sphere.
    B. the Infrared Astronomy Satellite.
    C. the naked eye.
    D. the radio telescope.

6. What literary technique does the author use in paragraph 3?

    A. alliteration
    B. onomatopoeia
    C. rhetorical questions
    D. personification

7. What is an example of the "magic places" referred to paragraph 9?

    A. the Earth
    B. a section of sky that has few stars
    C. the Sun
    D. the center of the galaxy

8. The author's attitude toward the search for extraterrestrial life can best be described as

    A. curious and excited.
    B. impatient and cynical.
    C. amused but indifferent.
    D. annoyed and puzzled.

OPEN-ENDED ITEM

9. In paragraphs 6–8, the author describes scientists'
    efforts to find solid evidence of extraterrestrial
    life.

    • What sorts of things are scientists looking for?
    • Explain why finding these things would be
      significant.

    Use information from the article to support your
    response.

_____

_____

_____

_____

_____

_____

_____

_____

_____

_____

_____

_____

_____

THE BASICS

You've probably heard the expression *read between the lines*. It means to understand something that is implied or suggested but not stated directly.

You "read between the lines" all the time, usually without even realizing it. For example, suppose you have a friend who makes only positive comments about her history teacher. Judging from your friend's apparent feelings, you'd probably conclude that she likes the teacher and is doing well in the class.

When you read between the lines, you take in information and combine it with knowledge that you already have. Based on this combination, you make inferences and draw conclusions. Because writers often imply their ideas rather than state them, making inferences is an important skill to have—and an essential skill for the Language Arts HSPA.

Reading Between the Lines

Combine...	with...	to make...
Ideas/information from a selection	your knowledge and experience	inferences and conclusions

Inferences and Conclusions

To *infer* means to combine information you read (or hear, if you're listening to a speaker) with your own knowledge, experience, and judgment to make an educated guess. When you make an *inference*, you reach an understanding or draw a conclusion that goes beyond what is directly stated. Your inference helps you figure out an author's implied ideas and understand the meaning of the selection.

You can make inferences about many different aspects of a selection. For example, when you read an essay, you may make inferences about the central idea, about implied main ideas, or about the author's purpose. When you read a short story, you may make inferences about theme, characters, or plot.

Inferences are based on ideas and supporting information. Because it's often possible to reach more than one conclusion, you have to use your judgment to make the inference that seems most reasonable in light of the information you have.

Activity D: Inferences and Conclusions

Read each example and answer the questions that follow.

> *Alice heard a crash. She ran to the kitchen. The cat was up on the counter. Scattered all over the floor were about 50 jagged pieces of what had been a crystal vase.*

1. What conclusion can you draw? Why?

_____

_____

_____

_____

_____

The gray sky abruptly lit up like a Fourth of July festival. There was a deafening boom. The lifeguards frantically blew their whistles. "Everyone out of the pool!" they yelled. "Now!"

2. Why are the lifeguards ordering people out of the pool? How did you determine your answer?

_____

_____

_____

_____

_____

The doorbell rang three times before Brian reluctantly pulled himself up from the couch and opened the door. He was in no mood for company. When he saw it was Ariel, he stared at her in disbelief. But just for an instant. "Maybe we should talk—," she began, just as Brian grabbed her and hugged her as tightly as he had ever hugged anyone in his life.

3. What can you infer from this brief passage? Explain your reasoning.

_____

_____

_____

_____

FYI Detective Work

Making inferences is like doing detective work. First, you look for clues. Then, using your knowledge and experience, you have to figure out what the clues mean.

Such detective work is especially important when you read narrative selections and poetry. In such selections, authors are more likely to suggest their meaning than to state it directly.

STRATEGIES

Use the strategies below to help you make inferences and draw conclusions. Remember that selections typically consist of stated *and* implied ideas. Be alert for both in order to fully understand the author's meaning.

Making Inferences and Drawing Conclusions

> ➤ **Consider how ideas and supporting information all fit together.**
> Making inferences is like putting together a jigsaw puzzle. Once all the pieces are in place, you can see the whole picture. This "picture" may be the central idea of a selection or the implied main idea of a paragraph. Suppose, for instance, that a selection describes several examples of people joining together to achieve a goal. What might the author be saying about the value of teamwork?
>
> Pay careful attention to details, too. For example, if someone's home is filled with trophies and sports posters, what can you infer about the person?

> ➤ **Look for connections between events.**
> What happened first? What happened next? Did one event cause, or result from, another? What event would you expect to happen next? For instance, suppose a young child finds a book of matches. Later, a fire breaks out in that child's home. What might you suspect about the cause of the fire?
>
> You can read more about how writers connect events in "Patterns of Development," on pages 70–72.

> ➤ **Ask *why*.**
> To draw a conclusion, ask yourself *why* someone acted as he/she did or *why* a situation developed or ended in a certain way. For example, a person who lies to spare someone else's feelings may be being kind. Someone who lies for personal gain is just dishonest.

> ➤ **Watch for comparisons.**
> Authors often make a point by showing how people or things are alike or different or how they have changed over time. For example, an author might describe a town as having "as much traffic and pollution as a big city."

> ➤ **Adjust inferences for new information.**
> Once you make an inference, watch for new information that confirms—or changes—your conclusion. This is especially important when you read fiction because authors introduce new information as they develop the plot.
>
> Here's an example. A character in a story is arrested for burglary. From the evidence, it appears that she is guilty. However, as you read on, details suggest that the character may be covering up for the true criminal, her best friend. You may need to change your conclusion.

➤ **Consider the author's choice of words.**

Authors convey their meaning and point of view through their choice of language. For example, compare the following sentences. How did changing two words significantly alter the meaning of the sentence?

Hernandez was a *daring* pilot who made *quick* decisions.

Hernandez was a *reckless* pilot who made *hasty* decisions.

 Denotation vs. Connotation

A word's *denotation* is its literal meaning—its dictionary definition. A word's *connotation* is its implied meaning.

Authors shape your interpretation of text by choosing words that have a positive or negative connotation. For example, *crowd* and *mob* both refer to a large group of people, but *mob* has a negative connotation.

Be especially alert for the connotation of words when you read persuasive or descriptive writing.

Activity E: Using the Strategies

Read the following brief selection and answer the questions that follow.

Good Morning, Kids

It's Saturday morning. Across the nation, young children are sprawled in front of television sets. They're viewing their favorite programs, the ones they watch every Saturday and often during the week as well.

Images bombard these young viewers, fast-moving pictures filled with comic book colors and accompanied by blaring sounds. Crazed animated villains blow up buildings with ray guns or obliterate them with bombs. Evil super-robots demolish entire cities, as people run screaming through the streets. Cartoon characters pound one another with mallets, blast each other with shotguns, and fling each other off cliffs. Good guys do battle with bad guys, sometimes using fists and feet, other times using the latest in high-tech weaponry. The mayhem and murder are interrupted only by commercials selling action figures, fast food, and computer games.

Research studies have shown that some of the most popular children's programs are five times more violent than shows televised during prime time. Some years ago, one study even identified "Bugs Bunny—Roadrunner" as the single most violent program on television.

And adults wonder why children seem "desensitized" to violence and suffering in the real world, why kids sometimes respond with violence themselves. Spend an hour or two watching children's television, and the answer comes through as clearly as a gunshot.

1. (A)   What is the central idea of this selection?

   _____

   _____

   _____

(B)   Explain how you determined the central idea.

_____

_____

_____

_____

2.   (A)   What is the main idea of the second paragraph?

_____

_____

_____

(B)   Explain how you determined the main idea.

_____

_____

_____

_____

3.   How did the author's choice of language help to convey the author's meaning and point of view? Be specific.

_____

_____

_____

_____

Two-Step Approach to Inferential Questions

Chapter 2 (pages 18 and 19) discussed how certain key words and phrases may signal when a question asks you to make an inference. For some such inferential questions on the HSPA, you'll find it helpful to take a two-step approach.

Study the following examples. Both relate to nonfiction selections.

EXAMPLE A:

In a speech to a graduating class, the author might tell students to

A.   go to college.
B.   join the army.
C.   travel abroad.
D.   go to work.

This question asks you to infer what the author *might* say. Use this two-step approach:

Step 1: Determine from the selection the author's main ideas.
Step 2: Pick the choice that best reflects these ideas.

EXAMPLE B:

Which of the following would the author most likely favor?

A. higher taxes

B. lower taxes

C. no taxes at all

D. taxes only on the rich

This question asks you to infer what the author *would . . . most likely* be in favor of. Again, use the two-step approach:

Step 1: Determine from the selection the author's main ideas.

Step 2: Pick the choice that best reflects these ideas.

Activity F: Inferential Questions

In your own words, summarize the two-step approach to answering inferential questions.

APPLYING YOUR KNOWLEDGE

1. Read the selection and answer the questions. Use the strategies that you've learned in this chapter *and* in Chapter 2.

2. After you've finished, read "Thinking It Through" to see how one student answered the questions.

Sometimes it can take many years to achieve a personal goal. In the following article, writer Sandra Cisneros describes her experience with her father.

Only Daughter
by Sandra Cisneros

1   Once, several years ago, when I was just starting out my writing career, I was asked to write my own contributor's note for an anthology I was part of. I wrote: "I am the only daughter in a family of six sons. *That* explains everything."

2   Well, I've thought about that ever since, and yes, it explains a lot to me, but for the reader's sake I should have written: "I am the only daughter in a *Mexican* family of six sons." Or even: "I am the only daughter of a Mexican father and Mexican-American mother." Or: "I am the only daughter of a working-class family of nine." All of these had everything to do with who I am today.

3   I was/am the only daughter and *only* a daughter. Being an only daughter in a family of six sons forced me by cir-cumstance to spend a lot of time by myself because my brothers felt it beneath them to play with a *girl* in public. But that aloneness, that loneliness, was good for a would-be writer—it allowed me time to think and think, to imagine, to read and prepare myself.

4   Being only a daughter for my father meant my destiny would lead me to become someone's wife. That's what he believed. But when I was in the fifth grade and shared my plans for college with him, I was sure he understood. I remember my father saying, "*Que bueno, ni' ja,* that's good." That meant a lot to me, especially since my brothers thought the idea hilarious. What I didn't realize was that my father thought college was good for girls—good for finding a husband. After four years in college and two more in graduate school, and still no husband, my father

shakes his head even now and says I wasted all that education.

In retrospect, I'm lucky my father believed daughters were meant for husbands. It meant it didn't matter if I majored in something silly like English. After all, I'd find a **5** nice professional eventually, right? This allowed me the liberty to putter about embroidering my little poems and stories without my father interrupting with so much as a "What's that you're writing?"

But the truth is, I wanted him to interrupt. I wanted my father to understand what it was I was scribbling, to intro-**6** duce me as "My only daughter, the writer." Not as "This is only my daughter. She teaches." *Es maestra*—teacher. Not even *profesora*.

In a sense, everything I have ever written has been for him, to win his approval even though I know my father can't read English words, even though my father's only reading includes the brown-ink *Esto* sports magazine from Mexico City and the bloody *¡Alarma!* magazines that feature **7** yet another sighting of *La Virgen de Guadalupe* on a tortilla or a wife's revenge on her philandering husband by bashing his skull in with a *molcajete* (a kitchen mortar made of volcanic rock). Or the *fotonov-elas*, the little picture paperbacks with tragedy and trauma erupting from the characters' mouths in bubbles.

My father represents, then, the public majority. A public who is uninter-**8** ested in reading, and yet one whom I am writing about and for, and privately trying to woo.

When we were growing up in Chicago, we moved a lot because of **9** my father. He suffered bouts of nostalgia. Then we'd have to let go our flat, store the furniture with mother's relatives, load the station wagon with baggage and bologna sandwiches and head south. To Mexico City.

We came back, of course. To yet another Chicago flat, another Chicago neighborhood, another Catholic school. **10** Each time, my father would seek out the parish priest in order to get a tuition break, and complain or boast: "I have seven sons."

He meant *siete hijos*, seven children, but he translated it as "sons." "I have seven sons." To anyone who would lis-**11** ten. The Sears Roebuck employee who sold us the washing machine. The short-order cook where my father ate his ham-and-eggs breakfasts. "I have seven sons." As if he deserved a medal from the state.

My papa. He didn't mean anything by that mistranslation, I'm sure. But somehow I could feel myself being erased. **12** I'd tug my father's sleeve and whisper: "Not seven sons. Six! and *one daughter*."

When my oldest brother graduated from medical school, he fulfilled my father's dream that we study hard and use this—our heads, instead of this—our hands. Even now my father's hands are thick and yellow, stubbed by a his-**13** tory of hammer and nails and twine and coils and springs. "Use this," my father said, tapping his head, "and not this," showing us those hands. He always looked tired when he said it.

Wasn't college an investment? And hadn't I spent all those years in college? And if I didn't marry, what was it all for? Why would anyone go to college and then choose **14** to be poor? Especially someone who had always been poor.

Last year, after ten years of writing professionally, the financial rewards started to trickle in. My second National Endowment for the Arts Fellowship. A guest professor-**15** ship at the University of California, Berkeley. My book, which sold to a major New York publishing house.

At Christmas, I flew home to Chicago. The house was throbbing, same as always; hot *tamales* and sweet *tamales* hissing in my mother's pressure cooker, and everybody—my mother, **16** six brothers, wives, babies, aunts, cousins—talking too loud and at the same time, like in a Fellini film, because that's just how we are.

I went upstairs to my father's room. One of my stories had just been translated into Spanish and published in an anthology of Chicano writing, and I wanted to show it to him. **17** Ever since he recovered from a stroke two years ago, my father likes to spend his leisure hours horizontally. And that's how I found him, watching a Pedro Infante movie on Galavisión and eating rice pudding.

There was a glass filmed with milk on the bedside table. There were several vials of pills and balled Kleenex. And on the floor, one black sock and a plastic urinal that I did-**18** n't want to look at but looked at anyway. Pedro Infante was about to burst into song, and my father was laughing.

I'm not sure if it was because my story was translated into Spanish, or because it was published in Mexico, or per-**19** haps because the story dealt with Tepeyac, the *colonia* my father was raised in and the house he grew up in, but any rate, my father punched the mute button on his remote control and read my story.

20 I sat on the bed next to my father and waited. He read it very slowly. As if he were reading each line over and over. He laughed at all the right places and read lines he liked out loud. He pointed and asked questions: "Is this So-and-so?" "Yes," I said. He kept reading.

When he was finally finished, after what seemed like hours, my father looked up and asked: "Where can we get **21** more copies of this for the relatives?"

Of all the wonderful things that happened to me last year, **22** that was the most wonderful.

1. In the last paragraph, the author writes, "Of all the wonderful things that happened to me last year, that was the most wonderful." What does she mean by this statement?

   A. She is looking forward to seeing her relatives from Mexico.
   B. She is pleased because her father can now read.
   C. She is happy that her father finally appreciates her as a writer.
   D. She realizes that her writing will probably make her rich.

2. The author's father wanted his daughter to

   A. get married.
   B. become a writer.
   C. go to graduate school.
   D. move to Mexico.

3. According to the author, being "the only daughter in a Mexican family of six sons" (paragraph 2) meant that

   A. less was expected of her.
   B. she could not go to college.
   C. she was smarter than her brothers.
   D. her father did not love her.

4. Which quotation BEST summarizes the author's feelings about her father's attitude as she was growing up?

   A. "My father represents . . . the public majority."
   B. ". . . I know my father can't read English words. . ."
   C. "He suffered bouts of nostalgia."
   D. ". . . somehow I could feel myself being erased."

5. The author's tone when writing about her father can BEST be described as

   A. angry and resentful.
   B. frustrated but understanding.
   C. amused and entertained.
   D. frightened and confused.

6. With which of the following statements would the author most likely agree?

   A. Men and women deserve equal opportunities.
   B. Men should be taken more seriously than women.
   C. A woman's goal in life should be to get married.
   D. Fathers do not make good parents.

Thinking It Through

1. In the last paragraph, the author writes, "Of all the wonderful things that happened to me last year, that was the most wonderful." What does she mean by this statement?

   A. She is looking forward to seeing her relatives from Mexico.
   B. She is pleased because her father can now read.
   C. She is happy that her father finally appreciates her as a writer.
   D. She realizes that her writing will probably make her rich.

   I realize that this question relates to the theme of the article: the author's desire to win her father's approval and recognition. There are key clues to the answer in paragraphs 6 and 7. In paragraph 6, the author describes how she wanted her father to recognize her as a writer. And in paragraph 7, she explains that "everything I have ever written has been for him, to win his approval." When her father reads and enjoys the story and asks for "more copies of this for the relatives" (paragraph 21), he is at last expressing approval, which delights the author. The correct answer is choice C.

2. The author's father wanted his daughter to

   A. get married.
   B. become a writer.
   C. go to graduate school.
   D. move to Mexico.

I know from the article that choice A is correct, but I consider the other choices just to make sure. I know that choice B is wrong, and choices C and D are not supported by the text. Therefore, I'm confident that choice A is right.

3. According to the author, being "the only daughter in a Mexican family of six sons" (paragraph 2) meant that

   A. less was expected of her.
   B. she could not go to college.
   C. she was smarter than her brothers.
   D. her father did not love her.

I know from the text that the father's main concern was that his daughter find a husband. For example, in paragraph 4 she explains that: "Being only a daughter for my father meant my destiny would lead me to become someone's wife." I know choice B is wrong, and choices C and D are not supported by the article. I can safely conclude that choice A is the correct answer.

4. Which quotation BEST summarizes the author's feelings about her father's attitude as she was growing up?

   A. "My father represents . . . the public majority."
   B. ". . . I know my father can't read English words. . ."
   C. "He suffered bouts of nostalgia."
   D. ". . . somehow I could feel myself being erased."

Like question 1, this question too relates to the theme of the article. Choice D, which comes from paragraph 12, best summarizes the author's feelings.

5. The author's tone when writing about her father can BEST be described as

   A. angry and resentful.
   B. frustrated but understanding.
   C. amused and entertained.
   D. frightened and confused.

Despite her frustration, the author makes clear that she understands her father's feelings. For example, in paragraph 12, she writes: "My papa. He didn't mean anything by that mistranslation, I'm sure." Choice B is the correct answer.

6. With which of the following statements would the author most likely agree?

   A. Men and women deserve equal opportunities.
   B. Men should be taken more seriously than women.
   C. A woman's goal in life should be to get married.
   D. Fathers do not make good parents.

For this kind of inferential question I use the two-step approach. First, I determine the author's main ideas. Then I pick the choice that best reflects these ideas. Based on this article, I know that the author would be most likely to agree with the first statement, but none of the others. Choice A is the correct answer.

REVIEW

Here's a brief summary of what you've learned in section 3.2. To review any of these points in detail, turn to the pages shown.

The basics (pages 60–61):
   → To *infer* means to combine information you read or hear with your own knowledge, experience, and judgment to make an educated guess.
   → When you make an *inference*, you reach an understanding or draw a conclusion that goes beyond what is directly stated.
   → Making inferences helps you figure out an author's implied ideas.
   → Because it's often possible to reach more than one conclusion, you have to use your judgment to make the inference that seems most reasonable.

Making inferences and drawing conclusions (pages 62–64):
   → Consider how ideas and supporting information all fit together.
   → Look for connections between events.
   → Ask *why*.
   → Watch for comparisons.
   → Adjust inferences for new information.
   → Consider the author's choice of words.

Two-step approach to inferential questions (pages 64–65):
   → First determine from the selection the author's main ideas. Then pick the choice that best reflects these ideas.

PATTERNS OF DEVELOPMENT

Authors develop their content in various ways. For example, the box on page 51 described three common methods of organizing ideas and information: order of increasing importance/interest, order of decreasing importance/interest, and chronological (time) order.

There are many other ways to organize and develop the paragraphs of a selection and/or the ideas within a paragraph. The particular approach an author chooses depends on the content and on the author's purpose.

Cause and effect

Cause-and-effect relationships appear in all kinds of selections. For example, novels show the consequences of characters' actions. News articles and essays describe how present-day events lead to or result from other events. Nonfiction books analyze the causes and effects of historical events.

A *cause* is something that produces an effect or makes something happen. A cause may take many different forms. It may be an action, an event, a situation, or a reason.

An *effect* is a result or consequence brought about by a cause. Even though a cause always occurs before an effect, writers may present the effect first.

Examples:

> *A gust of wind knocked down the sign.*
> wind (cause) → sign knocked down (effect)
>
> *The voters' disapproval of the governor led to a Democratic victory.*
> voters' disapproval (cause) → Democratic victory (effect)
>
> *The victim died as a result of the car accident.*
> car accident (cause) → victim's death (effect)
>
> *Lee worked hard and earned high grades.*
> working hard (cause) → earning high grades (effect)
>
> *Toni was so thirsty, she drank two glasses of water.*
> thirst (cause) → drinking water (effect)

A cause may produce one effect or several effects. Furthermore, an effect may result from one cause or from a combination of causes. Examples:

> One cause, two effects:
> *Because of the rain, the game was cancelled and we went home.*

Two causes, one effect:
Because of the rain and the strong winds, the game was cancelled.

Writers often use cause and effect to organize ideas and information. For example, a writer may describe an effect in the first paragraph of an essay and then explain the causes in the following paragraphs.

Cause-and-effect relationships may be direct or indirect. For example, a magazine article may describe how a drought is damaging farmers' crops in a small town. The loss of crops, in turn, is forcing farmers to take second jobs to earn additional income. As a result, teenagers in the town are finding fewer part-time work opportunities. In this way, the drought is having both direct and indirect effects.

Causes and effects may be stated or implied. In persuasive and informational writing, they are usually stated. However, in literary works you often have to make inferences. For example, you may have to infer the reasons behind a character's actions.

Words that May Signal Cause and Effect

because	*as a result*	*consequence*	*why*
since	*result in*	*therefore*	*consequently*
thus	*due to*	*so*	*so that*
if . . . then	*reason*	*nevertheless*	*produce*

Comparison/contrast

When you *compare* persons, places, or things, you look for similarities between them. For example, a comparison of two New Jersey communities would point out ways in which they are alike.

When you *contrast* persons, places, or things, you look for differences between them. For example, a writer contrasting northern New Jersey with southern New Jersey would identify ways in which the two parts of the state differ.

On the HSPA, comparison/contrast may appear in any of several ways.

- *As an underlying structure*: A writer may compare or contrast ideas, people, or objects. The writer may develop the comparison in a single paragraph or extend it for a page or more.

    Example: an essay comparing today's clothing styles with styles of the 1960s

- *As a literary element or technique*: A writer may make a comparison through the use of a simile, metaphor, or other literary device.

    Example: a paragraph comparing the government to a storm-tossed ship at sea

- *As a basis for analysis*: A multiple-choice or open-ended question may ask you to identify a comparison in a selection, make your own comparison, or explain the purpose served by a comparison. Extended writing tasks on the HSPA may also call on your ability to make comparisons.

    Example: a question asking you to compare the perspectives of characters in a story

Keep in mind that authors often communicate ideas through *implied* comparisons. Suppose, for example, a man and a woman in a story come upon an injured cat in the street. The man ignores the cat completely, but the woman stops to help the animal. What might their different reactions suggest about the two characters?

Words that May Signal Comparison/Contrast

similar	*different*	*similarity*	*difference*
alike	*both*	*like*	*as*
resembles	*opposite*	*however*	*on the other hand*
but	*although*	*even though*	*on the contrary*

Sequence

Sequence refers to the order in which writers present facts, details or events. The most common sequence is chronological order, in which a writer tells what happened first, what happened next, and what happened after that.

However, writers don't always follow time order. For example, a writer may begin by describing an incident—either fiction or nonfiction—and then tell about events leading up to that incident. Or, the author of a personal narrative may recall events that occurred at various times in his/her life. Sometimes writers jump around in time. They may alternate between present and past or insert brief flashbacks.

Words that May Signal Sequence

after	*before*	*first, second, etc.*	*afterward*
last	*later*	*next*	*then*
yesterday	*today*	*tomorrow*	*subsequently*

PRACTICE

The activities that follow will give you a chance to practice the strategies that you've learned in this chapter and in Chapter 2. Because HSPA questions call for a combination of skills, some practice questions touch on skills covered in other parts of this book.

Practice Activity 1

Read the selection and answer the multiple-choice and open-ended questions that follow.

Reminder: Use the strategies that you learned in this chapter *and* in Chapter 2.

There's an old saying that "appearances may be deceiving." The author explores the meaning of this saying in the following short story.

The Interrogation
by Eric Weiner

The headmistress opened her office door wide. She stared out at the slump-shouldered girl who sat stranded on the wide leather sofa of the outer office, waiting for her. The headmistress smiled without warmth. "Come in," she said.

It wasn't an invitation, it was an order. The girl got up. She gathered the books she had piled beside her on the sofa and, cradling them against her chest as if for protection, filed past the headmistress into the room.

3 The headmistress's office at the Hadley School for Girls looked as if it had been designed specifically to wring confessions from students. Walnut wainscoting and a paneled wooden ceiling made the room dark and <u>foreboding</u>. Large oil portraits of former headmistresses, all of whom seemed to stare down accusingly, hung on the walls. At the far end of the room loomed the headmistress's wide mahogany desk, dominating the entire space like a judge's platform. Across from the desk stood a high-backed wooden chair, floating alone in a sea of red

Oriental carpet. This was the seat for students who must face the headmistress. This was the seat of the accused.

"Sit down," the headmistress said curtly.

The girl sat. She was fifteen and in her third year at Hadley but she was a mousy sort of girl who made little impression. Miss Kendrick, the headmistress, only vaguely recognized her.

"I presume you know why you're **6** here."

The girl shook her head no.

"Oh, come now," the headmistress scoffed. She leaned against her desk, arms folded. "You didn't hear about the trouble with Mr. Carr?"

The girl squirmed. "I haven't heard a thing," she said. Behind her glasses, she kept blinking.

Miss Kendrick stared at the girl.

"I haven't," the girl insisted. But even as she said it, her heart was pounding out the words *I have, I have, I have.*

Every girl at Hadley already knew about the picture in Mr. Carr's classroom.

It showed Mr. Carr and the headmistress locked together in a wild position, which was probably physically impossible. Both figures were stark naked, and certain parts of their bodies had been drawn crudely out of proportion. And just in case the picture might seem to lack the old school spirit, the artist had added the Hadley school insignia as a tattoo on Mr. Carr's—.

The girl lowered her gaze to the red carpet. Not only did she know about the picture, she thought the picture was very funny. But she wasn't about to say so.

Miss Kendrick sat down. Her chair was larger than the girl's, and a little higher. "Well then," she said, "I guess you're the last to know." She smiled briefly. "It seems that someone has painted an obscenity in Mr. Carr's classroom. Mr. Carr is understandably upset. And deeply hurt. As am I."

"I'm sorry to hear that," the girl said, shifting in her seat.

"Are you?"

"Yes, ma'am." The girl started biting her nails, then quickly put her hand back under her books in her lap.

"Well, let me tell you why I'm so concerned," the headmistress said. "You know about the term *in loco parentis*?"

The girl did. In fact, it seemed to her it was all they ever talked about at Hadley. *In loco parentis*, "in the place of a parent." What it meant was there was always someone at Hadley telling you what to do.

"While you are within these walls," the headmistress intoned in her deep voice, "we are responsible for you girls in every way. From the moment you wake up to the moment you go to bed, it's our job to see that you are educated physically, spiritually, mentally, and morally. To do that, it is imperative that we command your utmost respect. Understood?"

"Yes, ma'am."

The headmistress placed her hands on the glossy wood of her desktop and pushed herself slowly to her full majestic height. She began pacing the room, circling around the girl. The girl could feel sweat beading on her upper lip. But she kept her hands under the books on her lap.

"Now. We know the picture was done during third period, because that's the only time Mr. Carr's classroom is idle.

We've talked to almost every girl who has third period free. You're second to last."

The girl blinked nervously, gave a little smile. "I'm used to that," she said.

Miss Kendrick didn't smile back. "Are you?" she asked. She was by the window now. She turned her back on the girl. Outside, it was a dingy November afternoon and the girl could see one of her dormmates making her way through the quad, looking cold, forlorn, and depressed. Probably on an errand for some senior, the girl thought.

Miss Kendrick's next question sounded almost casual, "Did you do it?"

It took the girl a second to respond. "No!" Her voice was raspy with tension.

The headmistress sighed. "I didn't think so. It seems that nobody did." She chuckled dryly as she sat down again. "I guess that picture just painted itself."

The headmistress fixed the girl with her pale gray eyes. "Where were you third period?"

"I . . . I . . . I don't want to say."

"You don't want to say? What are you talking about?"

"I . . . I just can't say, I'm sorry."

"You can't." Smiling, the headmistress glanced around the room as if she were sharing a joke with the paintings on the walls. "Good. So then you admit you painted the picture?"

"No!"

"Then where were you?"

The girl didn't answer.

The headmistress stared at the books on the girl's lap. "Put your books down," she ordered.

The girl's hands were shaking as she transferred the books to the carpet. She shoved her hands into the side pockets of her school uniform's plaid skirt.

The headmistress studied her for several moments, until the girl shivered. "All right," the headmistress said. "Let me see your hands."

"My what?"

"You heard me. Your hands. Let me see them."

At first the girl didn't move. Then she drew her hands out of her pockets. For a moment, she kept them in her lap palms down. Then slowly, reluctantly, the girl raised her hands.

"Closer!"

The girl stretched her hands out toward the desk. The headmistress leaned forward.

The girl's palms were spattered with black paint.

Miss Kendrick looked up slowly, her eyes boring into those of the girl. The girl looked down at her hands.

Then she started crying, large tears rolling down her cheeks. "OK, I admit it," she said softly, "I painted it, I painted it! OK? I painted the picture."

"You did."

"Y—yes."

"You're sure?"

"Yes! Yes!"

"You snuck in there and painted it?"

"Right."

"And that's why your hands are covered with black paint, is that correct?"

"Yes! Yes! That's what I'm saying! I painted that awful picture!" The girl's eyes were blurry with tears.

"Now why would someone do such a thing?" Miss Kendrick asked.

The girl snuffled loudly as she wiped her nose with the back of her hand. "I don't know. I guess I thought it would be funny."

"Funny? You call that filth funny?"

"Well, no, I don't, not anymore. I'm sorry. I really am." The girl waited, but the headmistress didn't say anything, so the girl said it again. "What else can I say? I'm really, really sorry."

"You are."

"Yes, ma'am."

The headmistress shook her head slowly, gravely. "OK, let's have it," she said. "What's going on?"

"What do you mean?"

"Why are you lying to me?"

"I don't know what—"

"Your hands are the wrong color."

"What? I don't under—"

"That little obscenity in Mr. Carr's classroom . . . it was painted in red."

The girl was about to speak, but she closed her mouth, swallowing the words.

"*All* red," the headmistress said.

The girl could feel her face flushing deeply. The headmistress's face reddened as well. They stared at one another. Then, abruptly, the girl started crying again. They were noisy sobs this time. "I'm . . . sorry," she struggled to say. "Oh, God. I'm sorry. I didn't mean . . . to lie."

"We'll deal with that later," the headmistress said. Her tone was almost gentle now. "Right now we just want to know who did it."

"But I . . . I can't!"

"Oh now, of course you can," said Miss Kendrick. The gentleness disappeared as abruptly as it had come. "I want the name. Now."

A last tear ran down into the corner of the girl's mouth. "If I tell, she won't get—suspended. Will she?"

"That's not your concern."

The girl looked down at her hands, studying her black stained fingers. "Laura did it," she said at last.

"Laura who?" the headmistress demanded, though there was only one Laura the girl could mean.

"Laura Templeton," the girl said. She covered her mouth, apparently horrified by what she had done. "Oh, God," she said, "I shouldn't have told, I—"

"Of course you should have," Miss Kendrick snapped. Her eyes were flashing. She was obviously stunned. "Well, come on," she said. "Let's have the rest of it."

"No, I can't, I—"

The headmistress snapped her fingers hard—twice—as if she were commanding a small animal. "Stop your whining," she ordered. The girl was silent. "Why did Laura Templeton paint that picture?"

"Well, she just did it for a gag, you know. She never thought Mr. Carr would get so mad. She really didn't—"

The girl gave the headmistress a pleading look, but Miss Kendrick's face offered her no hope.

"And?" Miss Kendrick asked.

"Well, when Mr. Carr got so furious, Laura got really scared. And she told me—" The girl hesitated.

"She told you what?"

"She told me that if I didn't take the blame for it, she'd fix it so"—a fresh sob escaped her—"so no girl ever talked to me again."

"I see."

Laura Templeton was a student Miss Kendrick knew and liked. She was pretty, popular, athletic. This year, as a senior, she'd been appointed proctor of Bingham Dorm. Proctors were in charge of checking that the other students observed all dorm rules. From everything that Miss Kendrick had heard, Laura was handling the job beautifully.

"I know, I know it doesn't seem like her," the girl said. "But . . . " She trailed off.

"But what? Listen, young lady, we're going to sit here until I've heard everything, so you can save yourself a lot of time and trouble by telling me exactly what is going on!"

The girl sighed. "It's like we're her slaves," she said quietly.

"Slaves? What kind of nonsense is this? She's only a proctor."

The girl nodded. "If she wants to, she can make your life a living . . . well . . . hell," the girl said.

"Go on," the headmistress ordered. "I want to hear it all."

The girl did as she was told. She told all, all the things the faculty didn't know about Laura. How Laura demanded

total respect. And if you crossed her, she would get you. Laura and her friends would shortsheet your bed. Knock your books out of your arms when they passed you on the paths. Spill coffee on your homework. Reset your alarm clock so you'd be late for class. If Laura was really angry with someone, she'd get the whole dorm chanting that girl's name before assembly.

Hearing this last item, the headmistress reddened again. She had heard plenty of chanting this year at assembly, and she had never managed to stop it.

"A lot of it's just little stuff, you know?" the girl continued. "But it kind of adds up. And, and if you want to get back in her good graces? Well, it's like, you have to be Laura's maid. And you have to do all these favors for her. It doesn't matter what she asks you, you have to do it and—"

The girl stopped short as if she had just realized where her words had taken her.

"And that's what happened to you," the headmistress said.

The girl nodded, blinking back fresh tears.

"So now you had to do her *this* favor, confessing to a crime you didn't commit?"

She nodded again.

Miss Kendrick thought for several moments. "All right," she said at last. "You can go."

She walked the girl to the door. Before she opened the door, Miss Kendrick told her she should keep their discussion private for the time being. The girl promised that she would. Then the headmistress opened the door and said, "Laura, you may come in now."

Laura Templeton was sitting and waiting on the same sofa where the girl herself had waited. The girl stopped short when she saw her.

Laura stood, smiling brightly at Miss Kendrick.

As much as the girl hated Laura, the sight of her caused her a sharp stab of remorse.

Then the girl left. Her heart was pounding like crazy.

At one-thirty that night, long after all the other young residents in Bingham Dorm had gone to sleep, the girl was still wide awake. She slipped out of her room and went softly down the hall to the bathroom.

The bathroom was deserted. Still, the girl was taking no chances. She took off her robe and stepped into one of the two shower stalls, which had the privacy of a curtain. She turned the faucets on full blast.

114 That afternoon, the dorm head had searched Laura's room and found a red-stained paintbrush. Rumor had it that she was going to be expelled.

The girl carefully scrubbed her hands. The black paint ran down her legs and swirled down the little metal drain.

Then she went to work on the red stains underneath.

1. The word **foreboding** as it is used in paragraph 3 means

   A. menacing.
   B. peaceful.
   C. enthusiastic.
   D. deceptive.

2. Which of the following is an example of a metaphor, a literary device used in the story?

   A. "The headmistress placed her hands on the glossy wood of her desktop and pushed herself slowly to her full majestic height."
   B. "The girl gave the headmistress a pleading look, but Miss Kendrick's face offered her no hope."
   C. Across from the desk stood a high-backed wooden chair, floating alone in a sea of red Oriental carpet."
   D. "Smiling, the headmistress glanced around the room as if she were sharing a joke with the paintings on the walls."

3. The girl's MAIN intent during the interrogation is to

   A. confess her crime.
   B. prove her innocence.
   C. get the headmistress to like her.
   D. place blame on Laura.

4. How might the girl's feelings toward Laura Templeton BEST be summarized?

   A. The girl wanted to get even with her.
   B. The girl respected and admired her.
   C. The girl was determined to protect her.
   D. The girl did not understand her.

5. The person who most likely put the red-stained paintbrush (paragraph 114) in Laura's room was

   A. the headmistress.
   B. Laura herself.

   C. the dorm head.
   D. the girl.

6. In paragraph 98, the girl's description of "all the things the faculty didn't know about Laura" suggests that

   A. Laura is a truly outstanding student.
   B. the girl is probably the only student who dislikes Laura.
   C. the girl and Laura are close friends.
   D. Laura is not as wonderful as the headmistress may think.

7. Students at the school most likely regard the headmistress with

   A. curiosity.
   B. fear.
   C. affection.
   D. gratitude.

8. The final sentence of the story is significant because it

   A. reveals that the girl herself painted the picture.
   B. shows that the girl meant no harm.
   C. suggests that both the girl and Laura are innocent.
   D. makes clear that Laura is guilty of the crime.

OPEN-ENDED ITEM

9. The headmistress tells the girl, "We've talked to almost every girl who has third period free. You're second to last." The girl answers, "I'm used to that."

   • What does the girl's response suggest about the way she feels?
   • How might the girl have handled her feelings in a more positive way?

Use information from the selection to support your response.

_____
_____
_____
_____
_____
_____
_____
_____
_____
_____
_____
_____
_____
_____
_____

Practice Activity 2

Answer the following questions about "The Interrogation."

1. Three of the strategies that you learned for making inferences are listed below. For each one, tell how you applied the strategy to "The Interrogation."

   A. *Consider how ideas and supporting information all fit together.*

   _____
   _____
   _____
   _____

   B. *Ask why.*

   _____
   _____
   _____
   _____

C. *Adjust inferences for new information.*

_____

_____

_____

_____

_____

2. What is the main idea of paragraph 3?

_____

_____

3. What information does the author use to develop the main idea of paragraph 3?

_____

_____

_____

_____

4. What is the main idea of paragraph 98?

_____

_____

5. What information does the author use to develop the main idea of paragraph 114?

_____

_____

_____

_____

THE BASICS

As you read, you may come across a word or phrase whose meaning you either don't know or are not sure about. When that happens, you can use clues from the surrounding context to help you figure out the meaning.

For the Language Arts HSPA, being able to determine meaning from context is doubly important. First of all, you need to know what words mean to fully understand the ideas and information in a selection. Secondly, some questions on the HSPA specifically ask you to identify the meaning of a word or phrase. (For two examples, look back at question 4 on page 58 and question 1 on page 77.)

Context Clues

You can determine the meaning of a word or phrase by examining the context in which it appears. *Context* means the words that come before and after a particular word or phrase.

The context may consist of a few words, a whole sentence, or a paragraph or more. Occasionally, you may even need to consider an entire selection to infer word meaning.

Words may have different meanings in different contexts. One meaning may be *literal* (using words in their usual sense) while another is *figurative* (using words in an imaginative way to create an effect).

Compare the following sentences. How does context help you determine the meaning of *barked*?

> The dog <u>barked</u> at the stranger. (literal meaning)
> "Two more laps!" the coach <u>barked</u> at the team. (figurative meaning)

Many words have more than one definition. You can use context to figure out which definition applies in a sentence.

Compare the following examples. How does context help you determine the meaning of *bank* in each sentence?

> Liz was fishing from the <u>bank</u> of the river.
> Sam deposited money in the <u>bank</u>.

Activity G: Words with More than One Meaning

1. Think of two words that have both literal and figurative meanings. For each word, write a pair of sentences, one using the literal meaning, the other using the figurative meaning.

_____

_____

_____

_____

2. Think of two words that have more than one definition. For each word, write a pair of sentences showing the two definitions used in an appropriate context.

_____

_____

_____

_____

Activity H: Using Context

You can use your knowledge of language to infer the meaning of words. Read the poem "Jabberwocky" by Lewis Carroll on page 82. How does word context help you understand the poem?

_____

_____

_____

_____

_____

_____

_____

_____

_____

_____

FYI **Inferring Word Meanings**

When you use context to determine meaning, you're making an inference. That is, you're combining what you read or hear with your knowledge, experience, and judgment to make an educated guess. For more on making inferences, see section 3.2, "Making Inferences and Drawing Conclusions."

Jabberwocky
by Lewis Carroll

'Twas brillig, and the slithy toves
   Did gyre and gimble in the wabe;
All mimsy were the borogoves,
   And the mome raths outgrabe.

"Beware the Jabberwock, by son!
   The jaws that bite, the claws that
    catch!
"Beware the Jubjub bird, and shun
   The frumious Bandersnatch!"

He took his vorpal sword in hand:
   Long time the manxome foe he
    sought—
So rested he by the Tumtum tree,
   And stood awhile in thought.

And as in uffish though he stood,
   The Jabberwock, with eyes of
    flame,

Came whiffling through the tulgey wood,
   And burbled as it came!

One, two! One, two! And through and
   through
   The vorpal blade went snicker-snack!
He left it dead, and with its head
   He went galumphing back.

"And hast thou slain the Jabberwock?
   Come to my arms, my beamish boy!
O frabjous day! Callooh! Callay!"
   He chortled in his joy.

'Twas brillig, and the slithy toves
   Did gyre and gimble in the wabe;
All mimsy were the borogoves.
   And the mome raths outgrabe.

STRATEGIES

Use the following strategies to help you figure out the meaning of words and phrases. Call upon these strategies not just for the HSPA but whenever you are reading.

> ### ➤ Study the surrounding sentence(s).
> You can often figure out an unfamiliar word by thinking carefully about the sentence in which it appears, especially the words closest to the word. However, don't limit yourself to just one sentence. Look back or ahead several sentences—or even paragraphs—to find context clues.

    EXAMPLE:

    Mrs. Danders is our most <u>loquacious</u> neighbor. She speaks to anyone at any time for any reason. Furthermore, she continues speaking long after the listener has stopped paying attention.

    Loquacious means "very talkative." The second and third sentences provide descriptive information from which you can figure out the word's meaning.

> ### ➤ Look for examples.
> Authors often clarify the meaning of a word through examples.

    EXAMPLE:

    <u>Avarice</u> has become an illness of modern times. People are obsessed with money, with possessions. They fantasize about winning the lottery. They read countless get-rich-quick books. They dream of shiny new cars and elegant homes. They hunger for expensive clothes and priceless jewelry.

The writer's supporting information in this paragraph tells you that *avarice* means "greed."

➤ **Look for an opposite or contrast.**
Writers may reveal a word's meaning by using an opposite or contrasting word or phrase. Contrasts are often, but not always, signaled by such words as *but, however, not, although, unlike.*

> **EXAMPLE:**
>
> *Unlike our <u>lethargic</u> old dog, the puppy was full of energy.*

The word *unlike* signals that the writer is contrasting the old dog and the puppy. *Lethargic* means "lacking energy," in contrast to "full of energy."

➤ **Look for a comparison.**
Writers may suggest a word's meaning by making a comparison. Contrasts are often, but not always, signaled by such words as *like, as, resembling, similar.*

> **EXAMPLE:**
>
> *Carl's quitting the team was an <u>impetuous</u> act, like a child throwing a toy.*

Impetuous in this context means "done suddenly with little thought." The word *like* signals the comparison with a child's action.

➤ **Look for a synonym.**
A *synonym* is a word that means the same or almost the same as another word. A synonym can help you understand the meaning of an unfamiliar word.

> **EXAMPLE:**
>
> *Jean loved the <u>serenity</u> of the little village. Its calmness helped her forget her worries.*

Serenity and *calmness* are synonyms.

➤ **Look for an explanation or definition.**
Writers often explain or define a term when they introduce it.

> **EXAMPLE:**
>
> *Patients with back problems may benefit from <u>magnetic resonance imaging</u>, or MRI. This new technology produces a cross-section picture that physicians can use to make a proper diagnosis.*

The context explains the phrase "magnetic resonance imaging." Notice how the words *patients, physicians,* and *diagnosis* indicate a medical context.

➤ **Put *all* your knowledge to work.**
Combine your use of context clues with your knowledge of language. Memorize the meaning of common prefixes, suffixes, and word roots so that you can figure out word meanings. For example, if you know the Greek roots *geo* (earth) and *logy* (study of), you can figure out that *geology* is the study of the earth.

Try Out Your Answer

For multiple-choice questions that ask you to identify the meaning of a word or phrase, always try out your answer choice in context. That is, reread the sentence (or paragraph) to see if your definition makes sense. If it doesn't, reconsider the other choices.

APPLYING YOUR KNOWLEDGE

1. Read the selection and answer the questions. Use the strategies that you've learned in this chapter *and* in Chapter 2.

    Reminder: If you're not sure which answer is correct, narrow your search by eliminating choices you know are wrong. Then concentrate on just the remaining choices.

2. After you've finished, read "Thinking It Through" to see how one student answered the questions.

Thank You
by Alex Haley

1 It was 1943, during World War II, and I was a young U.S. coastguardsman, serial number 212–548, a number we never seem to forget. My ship, the USS *Murzim*, had been under way for several days. Most of her holds contained thousands of cartons of canned or dried foods. The other holds were loaded with five-hundred-pound bombs packed delicately in padded racks. Our destination was a big base on the island of Tulagi in the South Pacific.

I was one of the *Murzim*'s several cooks and, quite the same as for folk ashore, this Thanksgiving morning had seen us busily preparing a traditional dinner featuring roast turkey.

Well, as any cook knows, it's a lot of hard work to cook and serve a big meal, and clean up and put everything away. But finally, around sundown, with our whole galley crew just bushed, we finished at last and were free to go flop into our bunks in the fo'c'sle[1].

[1]Abbreviation of <u>forecastle</u>, the crew's quarters in a merchant ship's bow.

4 But I decided first to go out on the *Murzim*'s afterdeck for a breath of open air. I made my way out there, breathing in great, deep <u>draughts</u> while walking slowly about, still wearing my white cook's hat and the long apron, my feet sensing the big ship's vibrations from the deep-set, turbine diesels and my ears hearing that slightly hissing sound the sea makes in resisting the skin of a ship.

I got to thinking about Thanksgiving. In reflex, my thoughts registered the historic imagery of the Pilgrims, Indians, wild turkeys, pumpkins, corn on the cob and the rest.

Yet my mind seemed to be questing for something else—some way that I could personally apply to the waning Thanksgiving. It must have taken me a half hour to sense that maybe some key to an answer could result from reversing the word "Thanksgiving"—at least that suggested a verbal direction, "Giving thanks."

Giving thanks—as in praying, thanking God, I thought. Yes, of course. Certainly.

Yet my mind continued nagging me. Fine. But something else.

After awhile, like a dawn's brightening, a further answer did come—that there were people to thank, people who had done so much for me that I could never possibly repay them. The embarrassing truth was I'd always just accepted what they'd done, taken all of it for granted. Not one time had I ever bothered to express to any of them so much as a simple, sincere "Thank you."

At least seven people had been particularly and <u>indelibly</u> helpful to me. I realized, with a gulp, that about half of them had since died—so they were forever beyond any possible expression of gratitude from me. The more I thought about it, the more ashamed I became. Then I pictured the three who were still alive and, within minutes, I was down in the fo'c'sle.

10

Sitting at a mess table with writing paper and memories of things each had done, I tried composing genuine statements of heartfelt appreciation and gratitude to my dad, Simon A. Haley, a professor at the old AMNC (Agricultural Mechanical Normal College) in Pine Bluff, Arkansas, now a branch of the University of Arkansas; to my grandma, Cynthia Palmer, back in our little hometown of Henning, Tennessee; and to the Rev. Lonual Nelson, my grammar school principal, retired and living in Ripley, six miles north of Henning.

I couldn't even be certain if they would recall some of their acts of years past, acts that I vividly remembered and saw now as having given me vital training, or inspiration, or directions, if not all of these desirables rolled into one.

The texts of my letters began something like, "Here, this Thanksgiving at sea, I find my thoughts upon how much you have done for me, but I have never stopped and said to you how much I feel the need to thank you—" And briefly I recalled for each of them specific acts performed in my behalf.

For instance, something uppermost about my father was how he had impressed upon me from boyhood to love books and reading. In fact, this graduated into a family habit of after-dinner quizzes at the table about books read most recently and new words learned. My love of books never diminished and later led me toward writing books myself. So many times I have felt a sadness when exposed to modern children so <u>immersed</u> in the electronic media that they have little to no awareness of the wondrous world to be discovered in books.

14

I reminded the Reverend Nelson how each morning he would open our little country town's grammar school with a prayer over his assembled students. I told him that whatever positive things I had done since had been influenced at least in part by his morning school prayers.

In the letter to my grandmother, I reminded her of a dozen ways she used to teach me how to tell the truth, to be thrifty, to share, and to be forgiving and considerate of others. (My reminders included how she'd make me pull switches from a peach tree for my needed lesson.) I thanked her for the years of eating her good cooking, the equal of which I had not found since. (By now, though, I've reflected that those <u>peerless</u> dishes are most gloriously flavored with a pinch of nostalgia.) Finally, I thanked her simply for having sprinkled my life with stardust.

16

Before I slept, my three letters went into our ship's office mail sack. They got mailed when we reached Tulagi Island.

We unloaded cargo, reloaded with something else, then again we put to sea in the routine familiar to us, and as the days became weeks, my little personal experience receded. Sometimes, when we were at sea, a mail ship would rendezvous and bring us mail from home, which, of course, we accorded topmost priority.

Every time the ship's loudspeaker rasped, "Attention! Mail call!" two-hundred-odd shipmates came pounding up on deck and clustered about the raised hatch atop which two yeomen, standing by those precious bulging gray sacks, were alternately pulling out fistfuls of letters and barking successive names of sailors who were, in turn, hollering "Here! Here!" amid the jostling.

One "mail call" brought me responses from Grandma, Dad and the Reverend Nelson—and my reading of their letters left me not only astounded, but more humbled than before.

Rather than saying they would forgive that I hadn't previously thanked them, instead, for Pete's sake, they were thanking *me*—for having remembered, for having considered they had done anything so exceptional.

Always the college professor, my dad had carefully avoided anything he considered too sentimental, so I knew how moved he was to write me that, after having helped educate many young people, he now felt that his best results included his own son.

The Reverend Nelson wrote that his decades as a "simple, old-fashioned principal" had ended with grammar schools undergoing such swift changes that he had retired in self-doubt. "I heard more of what I had done wrong than what I did right," he said, adding that my letter had brought him welcome reassurance that his career had been appreciated.

A glance at Grandma's familiar handwriting brought back in a flash memories of standing alongside her white wicker rocking chair, watching her "settin' down" some letter to relatives. Frequently touching her pencil's tip to pursed lips, character by character, each between a short, soft grunt, Grandma would slowly accomplish one word, then the next, so that a finished page would consume hours. I wept over the page representing my Grandma's recent hours invested in expressing her loving gratefulness to me—whom she used to diaper!

Much later, retired from the Coast Guard and trying to make a living as a writer, I never forgot how those three "thank you" letters gave me an insight into something nigh mystical in human beings, most of whom go about yearning in secret for more of their fellows to express appreciation for their efforts.

I discovered in time that, even in the business world, probably no two words are more valued than "thank you," especially among people at stores, airlines, utilities and others that directly serve the public.

Late one night, I was one of a half-dozen passengers who straggled weary and grumbling off a plane that had been forced to land at the huge Dallas/Fort Worth Airport. Suddenly, a buoyant, cheerful, red-jacketed airline man waved us away from the regular waiting room seats, say-ing, "You sure look bushed. I know a big empty office where you can stretch out while you wait." And we surely did. When the weather improved enough for us to leave, "Gene Erickson" was in my notebook and, back home, I wrote the president of that airline describing his sensitivity and his courtesy. And I received a thank you!

I travel a good deal on lecture tours and I urge students especially to tell their parents, grandparents, and other living elders simply "thank you" for all they have done to make possible the lives they now enjoy. Many students have told me they found themselves moved by the response. It is not really surprising, if one only reflects how it must feel to be thanked after you have given for years.

Now, approaching Thanksgiving of 1982, I have asked myself what will I wish for all who are reading this, for our nation, indeed for our whole world—since, quoting a good and wise friend of mine, "In the end we are mightily and merely people, each with similar needs." First, I wish for us, of course, the simple common sense to achieve world peace, that being paramount for the very survival of our kind.

And there is something else I wish—so strongly that I have had this line printed across the bottom of all my stationery: *Find the good—and praise it.*

1. The word **draughts** in paragraph 4 means

    A. winds.
    B. breaths.
    C. aromas.
    D. sounds.

2. In paragraph 10, the author refers to people who had been "**indelibly** helpful to me." In this context, **indelibly** means

    A. scarcely.
    B. surprisingly.
    C. briefly.
    D. lastingly.

3. As used in paragraph 14, the word **immersed** means

    A. absorbed.
    B. wet.
    C. stimulated.
    D. educated.

4. As used in paragraph 16, the word **peerless** means

    A. priceless.
    B. tasty.
    C. unforgettable.
    D. unequaled.

5. The word **straggled** in paragraph 27 means

    A. ran.
    B. laughed.
    C. wandered.
    D. fell.

6. In paragraph 27, the author describes an airline employee as "**buoyant**." In this context, **buoyant** means

    A. unsinkable.
    B. blunt.
    C. merry.
    D. weightless.

7. What is the central idea of this essay?

    A. People need to work together toward world peace.
    B. People should more often express their thanks.
    C. People have forgotten why we celebrate Thanksgiving.
    D. People should express their gratitude in letters.

8. In paragraph 16, what does the author mean when he uses the phrase "flavored with a pinch of nostalgia"?

    A. made with many different spices
    B. prepared by a secret recipe
    C. made sweeter by fond memory
    D. cooked with the assistance of others

9. In paragraph 25, the author writes that most people "go about yearning in secret for more of their fellows to express appreciation for their efforts." Which of the following positions does this statement support?

    A. "Find the good—and praise it."
    B. "My love of books never diminished and later led me toward writing books myself."
    C. "In the end we are mightily and merely people, each with similar needs."
    D. "I wish for us . . . the simple common sense to achieve world peace."

Thinking It Through

1. The word **draughts** in paragraph 4 means

    A. winds.
    B. breaths.
    C. aromas.
    D. sounds.

    In the paragraph's first sentence, the author writes that he was going out on deck "for a breath of open air." So, the "great, deep draughts" he's breathing in must be breaths of fresh air. The correct answer is choice B.

2. In paragraph 10, the author refers to people who had been "**indelibly** helpful to me." In this context, **indelibly** means

    A. scarcely.
    B. surprisingly.
    C. briefly.
    D. lastingly.

    I know that "indelible" ink is ink that can't be removed, but the meaning here is more figurative. From the overall context, I infer that the author means the help he received had a lasting effect—in a sense, an effect that "can't be removed." Choice D is the correct answer.

3. As used in paragraph 14, the word **immersed** means

    A. absorbed.
    B. wet.
    C. stimulated.
    D. educated.

    The author probably wouldn't "have felt a sadness" if children were "stimulated" or "educated" by electronic media, so I can eliminate choices C and D. *Immerse* can mean "put into water," but clearly that meaning doesn't apply here. Choice A is the correct answer.

4. As used in paragraph 16, the word **peerless** means

   A. priceless.
   B. tasty.
   C. unforgettable.
   D. unequaled.

I know that the suffix *-less* means "without" (as in *hopeless* or *careless*), and I also know that a "peer" is an equal. So, I can infer that *peerless* means "without equal," or "unequaled." (I also notice that in the preceding sentence, the author talks about not finding "the equal" of his grandmother's cooking.) Choice D is the correct answer.

5. The word **straggled** in paragraph 27 means

   A. ran.
   B. laughed.
   C. wandered.
   D. fell.

"Weary and grumbling" passengers are unlikely to either run or laugh, so I can eliminate choices A and B. Choice D doesn't make sense here, so I conclude that *straggle* must mean "wander." To be sure, I try out that meaning in the context. It does seem to work fine, so I conclude that choice C is correct.

6. In paragraph 27, the author describes an airline employee as "**buoyant**." In this context, **buoyant** means

   A. unsinkable.
   B. blunt.
   C. merry.
   D. weightless.

Only "merry" makes sense in this context. I also notice that the sentence describing the employee contains a synonym: "cheerful." The correct answer is choice C.

7. What is the central idea of this essay?

   A. People need to work together toward world peace.
   B. People should more often express their thanks.
   C. People have forgotten why we celebrate Thanksgiving.
   D. People should express their gratitude in letters.

Although the author might agree with all the choices, only choice B expresses the whole essay's central idea—its principal point or underlying meaning.

8. In paragraph 16, what does the author mean when he uses the phrase "flavored with a pinch of nostalgia"?

   A. made with many different spices

   B. prepared by a secret recipe

   C. made sweeter by fond memory

   D. cooked with the assistance of others

   The author uses figurative language here to make his point. He's saying that he realizes that happy memories of his grandmother's cooking tend to make "those peerless dishes" even better. The correct answer is choice C.

9. In paragraph 25, the author writes that most people "go about yearning in secret for more of their fellows to express appreciation for their efforts." Which of the following positions does this statement support?

   A. "Find the good—and praise it."

   B. "My love of books never diminished and later led me toward writing books myself."

   C. "In the end we are mightily and merely people, each with similar needs."

   D. "I wish for us . . . the simple common sense to achieve world peace."

   The statement is about people wanting to feel appreciated. Although choice C seems somewhat related, only choice A is clearly supported by the statement. Choice A is the correct answer.

Activity I: Inferences and Context Clues

On a separate piece of paper, write a paragraph explaining how the strategies you've learned for making inferences are related to the strategies for using context. Support your answer with examples.

FYI Build Your Vocabulary

The more words you know, the more you will have at your command when you read, write, or speak. Here are a few suggestions to help you build your vocabulary:

- Read! Spend time every day reading newspapers, magazines, and/or books.

- When you read or hear an unfamiliar word, look it up in a dictionary. Don't just skip it.

- Keep a list of new words that you learn. Try to use them in written and oral communication.

- Look for other ways to expand your vocabulary. For example, use a word-a-day desk calendar or a vocabulary-builder study book.

REVIEW

Here's a brief summary of what you've learned in section 3.3. To review any of these points in detail, turn to the pages shown.

The basics (pages 80–81):

→ *Context* means the words that come before and after a particular word or phrase. You can figure out the meaning of a word or phrase by thinking about its context.

→ Context may consist of a few words, a whole sentence, or a paragraph or more.

→ Words may have different meanings in different contexts. Meanings may be *literal* (words used in their usual sense) or *figurative* (words used in an imaginative way to create an effect).

→ Many words have more than one definition. Context can help you figure out which definition applies.

Using context to determine meaning (pages 82–83):

→ Study the surrounding sentence(s).

→ Look for examples.

→ Look for an opposite or contrast.

→ Look for a comparison.

→ Look for a synonym.

→ Look for an explanation or definition.

→ Put *all* your knowledge to work.

PRACTICE

The activities that follow will give you a chance to practice the strategies that you've learned in this chapter and in Chapter 2. Because HSPA questions call for a combination of skills, some practice questions touch on skills covered in other parts of this book.

Practice Activity 1

Read the selection and answer the multiple-choice and open-ended questions that follow.

Reminder: Use the strategies that you learned in this chapter *and* in Chapter 2.

In this article, the author examines the challenge that scientists face in creating robots that can function independently.

Smart Skin

by Shawna Vogel

If we're ever to have the future promised to us by "The Jetsons,"[1] we're at the very least going to need personal robots that can serve us breakfast. But to do that robots will have to be able to sense the difference between a glass of orange juice and a soft-boiled egg, and to hold each with just enough pressure to keep it from either breaking or dropping to the floor. At the moment such a fine-tuned grip is beyond the capacity of any robot in existence.

Robots have no <u>innate</u> "feel" for the objects they are handling primarily because they lack one of our most useful sense organs: skin. That isn't to say they can't get a grip on things. Industrial robots can repeatedly pick up objects like carburetors by exerting a preprogrammed pressure on them. But robots capable of functioning autonomously will need a "smart skin" to sense whether they should, say, grasp a wrench more firmly or ease up their death grip on a tomato.

2

One of the most sophisticated approaches to this goal is being developed at the University of Pisa by Italian engineer Danilo De Rossi, who has closely modeled an artificial skin on the inner and outer layers of human skin: the dermis and epidermis. His flexible, multilayered sheathing even has the same thickness as human skin—roughly that of a dime.

De Rossi's artificial dermis is made of a water-swollen conducting gel[2] sandwiched between two layers of electrodes that monitor the flow of electricity through the squishy middle. Like the all-natural human version, this dermis senses the overall pressure being exerted on an object. As pressure deforms the gel, the voltage between the electrodes changes; the harder the object being pressed, the greater the deformation. By keeping tabs on how the voltage is changing, a skin-clad robot could thus distinguish between a rubber ball and a rock.

For resolving the finer details of surface texture, De Rossi has created an epidermal layer of sensor-studded sheets of plastic placed between thin sheets of rubber. The sensors are pinhead-size disks made of piezoelectric[3] substances, which emit an electric charge when subjected to pressure. These disks can sense texture as fine as the bumps on a braille manuscript.

Other researchers have developed texture-sensitive skins, but De Rossi's has a unique advantage. Because his disks respond to pressure from any direction—including forces pulling sideways across the surface of the skin—they can also sense friction. "No other sensor today can do that," says De Rossi. Most smart skins detect only pressure perpendicular to the surface and cannot feel lateral deformation. But a robot wearing De Rossi's skin could easily feel the tug from a sticky piece of tape or, conversely, sense an alarming lack of friction when a greased motor bearing is slipping from its grasp.

Either of De Rossi's layers could be used separately to meet the specialized needs of industrial robots, but he envisions them as parts of an integrated skin for multipurpose mechanical hands. At the moment, however, De Rossi faces a small dilemma: his two layers are incompatible. The water essential to the working of the dermis <u>invariably</u> short-circuits[4] the sensitive epidermis. De Rossi will need to separate the two layers, but no matter what material he chooses he will probably have to compromise among several ideals, such as extreme thinness, strength, and flexibility.

7

Even if he does manage to unite his layers, there will still be a number of hurdles to get over before a robot with artificial skin can become as <u>adept</u> as a human. Foremost among them is the basic question of how to coordinate all the tactile information transmitted. Robotics engineers still puzzle over how people use all the tactile messages conveyed by their hands to accomplish a feat as simple as threading a nut onto the end of a bolt.

8

---

[1]**"The Jetsons"**: animated-cartoon TV series of the 1960s about a family of the future.

[2]**conducting gel**: a soft, elastic substance having the properties of both a liquid and a solid, which conducts, or transmits, electricity.

[3]**piezoelectric** (pee-AY-zoh): causing small variations in tiny currents as a result of mechanical stress.

[4]**short-circuits** (verb): disrupt the flow of electricity by providing a shorter path.

1. In paragraph 2, when the author uses the phrase "smart skin," she means skin that

   A. can protect humans from heat and cold.
   B. will not crack under pressure.
   C. can detect the need for more or less pressure.
   D. can withstand an electrical charge.

2. As used in paragraph 2, the word **innate** means

   A. permanent.
   B. logical.
   C. forceful.
   D. built-in.

3. Which of the following best expresses the central idea of this article?

   A. Industrial robots need "smart skin" in order to perform tasks repeatedly.
   B. Scientists are trying to overcome the problems of designing "smart skin" for robots.
   C. Once scientists perfect it, "smart skin" will save many human lives.
   D. It is unlikely that scientists will ever develop "smart skin."

4. The word **adept** in paragraph 8 means

   A. dependable.
   B. skilled.
   C. intelligent.
   D. gentle.

5. What is the "unique advantage" of the artificial skin developed by Danilo De Rossi?

   A. It is sensitive to texture.
   B. It responds to pressure.
   C. It can sense friction.
   D. It enables robots to solve problems.

6. The term "smart skin" is an example of a literary technique called

   A. personification.
   B. allegory.
   C. hyperbole.
   D. onomatopoeia.

7. In paragraph 7, the author writes, "The water essential to the working of the dermis **invariably** short-circuits the sensitive epidermis." In this context, **invariably** means

   A. always.
   B. seldom.
   C. strongly.
   D. never.

8. The widespread use of "smart skin" would most likely give robots

   A. greater ability to solve mathematical problems.
   B. fewer moving parts.
   C. many more uses.
   D. a much longer operational life.

OPEN-ENDED ITEM

9. In paragraph 7, the author states that "De Rossi faces a small dilemma: his two layers are incompatible."

   • If De Rossi solves this dilemma, what challenges remain to be overcome?
   • If and when scientists do develop robots with "smart skin," what purposes might such robots serve?

   Use information from the article to support your response.

   _____

   _____

   _____

   _____

   _____

   _____

   _____

   _____

   _____

   _____

_____

_____

_____

_____

_____

_____

_____

_____

Practice Activity 2

Answer the following questions about "Smart Skin."

1. What important ideas does the first paragraph of the article introduce?

   _____

   _____

   _____

2. The author writes that De Rossi "modeled an artificial skin on the inner and outer layers of human skin" (paragraph 3). How does the author develop this statement? Use specific information from the article to support your answer.

   _____

   _____

   _____

   _____

   _____

   _____

   _____

   _____

3.4 UNDERSTANDING AN AUTHOR'S PURPOSE AND POINT OF VIEW

THE BASICS

Authors have a purpose in mind when they write. For example, they may want to describe real or imagined events, present information, or persuade readers to think in a certain way. Recognizing an author's purpose will help you understand and analyze the selections on the Language Arts HSPA.

Keep in mind that authors often accomplish more than one purpose at a time. For instance, a newspaper editorial may *inform* readers about a proposed tax increase while trying to *persuade* them to support the proposal.

Authors write to . . .

convey information

influence readers' thoughts and actions

tell about actual or imagined events

describe people, places, or objects

entertain readers

Purpose and Point of View

As authors accomplish their writing purpose, they usually reveal their point of view. Although purpose and point of view are closely related, they are not the same.

An author's *purpose* is his/her reason or goal for writing. An author's *point of view* is how the author feels about his/her topic or central idea. Purpose and point of view may be stated directly, or they may be implied.

Author's purpose ➡ the author's reason for writing

Author's point of view ➡ the author's feelings about the topic or central idea

---

 Another "Point of View"

Besides referring to how an author feels about his/her topic or central idea, the term "point of view" may also refer to how an author tells his/her story. For example, a story may be told in *first-person* point of view or *omniscient* (all-knowing) point of view. To learn more about this meaning of the term, see page 112 under "Point of view."

To achieve their purpose, authors include some ideas, facts, details, and examples and omit others. They decide how to organize their content. They choose particular words to describe people, places, and events. Through such carefully made decisions and choices, authors shape their work.

Exactly how purpose and point of view are connected varies with each selection. Study the examples in the following chart.

HOW ARE AUTHOR'S PURPOSE AND POINT OF VIEW LINKED?

Selection	Purpose	Point of View
essay	to argue that colleges should place less emphasis on SAT scores	The author feels that SATs unfairly discriminate against students who don't do well on standardized tests.
article	to explain how the Internet works and describe its many benefits	The author thinks that people don't fully understand how useful the Internet can be.
short story	to suggest that children today are forced to grow up too quickly	The author thinks that "kids should be kids" and should be allowed to enjoy the freedom of childhood.
poem	to describe the beauty of the night sky	The author feels that gazing at the stars has a calming effect, yet stirs the imagination.

Activity J: Casting a Favorable Light

An author is writing a descriptive article about the town of Afton. Here are some facts and details that the author could use:

_____ (1) Many residents of Afton are high school dropouts.

_____ (2) Afton offers easy access to main highways.

_____ (3) The town has been fighting an air pollution problem without much success.

_____ (4) Families new to Afton find themselves warmly welcomed.

_____ (5) Afton has somewhat more crime than neighboring towns.

_____ (6) The nearest hospital to Afton is more than a half hour away.

_____ (7) The town has an attractive business district, with many fine stores.

_____ (8) Afton's school system is highly rated for quality of education.

If the author likes Afton and wants to show the town in a positive light, which details would he/she probably include? If the author does not like Afton and wants to show the town negatively, which details would he/she include? In the space next to each detail, write *P* for positive or *N* for negative.

FACTS VS. OPINIONS

Writers use facts to develop their ideas and support their point of view. However, they often mix facts with opinions. Think critically about what you read and hear, so that you can separate fact from opinion.

A *fact* is something known to be true. Facts are based on information that can be verified (shown to be true). A statement of fact can be proved.

Fact: *Trenton, the capital of New Jersey, is located in the western part of the state.*

An *opinion* is a belief, judgment, or conclusion based on what someone thinks. A statement of opinion cannot be proved or disproved.

Opinion: *Millburn is the prettiest town in northern New Jersey.*

Opinions alone cannot prove a point because you can agree or disagree with an opinion. Authors must use facts and examples to support their opinions and prove their arguments.

When you read a statement of opinion, look for supporting information. Often the statement of opinion is the topic sentence of a paragraph and is followed by supporting information.

Opinion (topic sentence):
Legal restrictions on gun ownership should be tightened.

Supporting information:
Guns cause some 2,000 accidental deaths each year. More than half of the victims are under 19 years of age.

STRATEGIES

Use the strategies below to help you understand an author's purpose and point of view.

➤ **Identify the most important ideas in the selection.**
To know an author's purpose and point of view, you have to understand the most important ideas and information in the selection. Use the strategies you learned in sections 3.1 and 3.2 of this chapter.

➤ **Consider your reactions to the selection.**
As you're reading, be aware of your response. Are you learning interesting facts? Changing your opinion about an issue? Becoming amused or annoyed by the author's words? Your reactions may offer clues to the author's purpose.

➤ **Think about the author's motive for writing.**
After reading a selection, ask yourself what made the author write it. Did he/she intend to influence your opinion? Explain a concept? Entertain you? Describe a significant event?

➤ **Think about what's included *and* what's not.**
For example, a writer may describe how well a car handles and how attractive it is without saying anything about the cost of running and maintaining the car. What might that suggest about the author's purpose and point of view?

➤ **Think about how the author organized the content.**
How a writer organizes ideas and information generally shows what he/she thinks is most important. To review three common methods of organization, see the box on page 51.

➤ **Notice the author's choice of words.**
Language can show people and events in either a favorable or an unfavorable light. For example, someone who refuses to give up may be described as "determined" or as "stubborn," depending on the author's point of view.

➤ **Pay attention to literary elements and writing techniques.**
Authors reveal their feelings and opinions through the use of figurative language, repetition, exaggeration, and other techniques. You'll read about elements of fiction and nonfiction in section 3.5. To learn about some common persuasive techniques, read the box that appears on page 102.

 Feelings Behind the Words

An author's point of view is based on his/her personal beliefs, assumptions, judgments, and biases. For example, suppose that someone who is a passionate sports fan writes an article about a proposal to cut the high school sports budget. Given the person's enthusiasm for sports, it's likely that he/she would oppose the proposal as well as any individuals or groups who favor it. In this way, authors' personal feelings can directly or indirectly affect their writing.

Activity K: Recognizing Purpose and Point of View

Read an editorial in a newspaper or magazine. (Your teacher may assign one to the class.) Then answer the questions below.

Title of editorial: _____

Newspaper/magazine: _____

Date of publication: _____

1. Summarize the author's most important ideas.

   _____

   _____

   _____

   _____

   _____

2. Why do you think the author wrote the editorial?

   _____

   _____

3. How does the author feel about his/her topic or central idea? What makes you think so?

   _____

   _____

   _____

   _____

   _____

4. How can the above strategies help you understand the editorial writer's purpose and point of view? Give two examples.

   _____

   _____

   _____

   _____

   _____

   _____

   _____

1. Read the selection and answer the questions. Use the strategies that you've learned in this chapter *and* in Chapter 2.

2. After you've finished, read "Thinking It Through" to see how one student answered the questions.

In the following excerpt from his book, the author examines factors that cause eating disorders and discusses ideas for preventing these disorders.

Looking Good, Eating Right
by Charles A. Salter

How Does One Develop an Eating Disorder?

The causes of eating disorders are not always clear. There may be genetic or biochemical factors in some cases. There may be psychological problems from early childhood or the present (such as school or family conflicts) that trigger the problem. Often, the psychological trap that immediately precedes anorexic or bulimic behavior is the double pressure to enjoy life through food and yet remain ultra-slim.

Society all around us encourages self-indulgence in food and drink as one of the main ways to enjoy life. For example, almost any popular magazine, newspaper, or TV show has ads showing attractive food that makes your mouth water at first glance. The characters in movies and TV shows are often shown indulging themselves with a bewildering array of high-fat snacks and treats. In real life, no party or ceremonial event would be complete without a table full of tasty food items. To be part of the action, to be popular, you are supposed to eat, eat, eat. . . .

But in real life most people, if they keep consuming like that, just keep putting on more and more weight. They then find themselves in conflict with another dominant pressure in society—to stay slim and trim. Models in ads —even those hawking food—and actors in shows—even those shown gorging themselves on fatty foods—are usually physically fit and quite thin.

All of these incompatible pressures put teens in a terrible bind. A person with a very high metabolism rate may be able to overeat and not gain weight. But the vast majority of us are not so lucky. (Even people in the high-metabolism category usually find their rate slowing and their weight increasing over the years.) The "solution" that some teens choose is to deny themselves all the time so as

to keep temptation at bay. But soon, hunger and food boredom lead to a binge. Feeling guilty over the binge, they desperately seek a way out. For instance, they make themselves throw up or they double their resolve to eat less in the future. Over time they develop anorexia or bulimia.

Why do some teens develop eating disorders while others don't? Some experts relate the problem to childhood traumas, disturbed family relationships, chemical imbalances in the brain, or distorted self-images. But speculation about the causes often does not help much unless sufficient time is spent with a psychiatrist or psychologist to explore those causes thoroughly. Someone who already has a full-fledged eating disorder or has traumatic conflicts pushing him or her strongly toward unhealthy eating should consult a professional immediately.

Treatment of Eating Disorders

Once an eating disorder has become firmly established, there is no easy cure. Someone who's never suffered anorexia and never known an anorexic might be tempted to think, "It's simple—just tell them to eat more!"

Unfortunately, it's not that simple. Even when anorexics have been brought into the hospital and are receiving physical care, nutritional therapy, and psychiatric care, many don't improve much. Some will go to extraordinary lengths to deceive family members and doctors, pretending to change but not really doing so. Some others will begin to improve under the intense scrutiny possible in a hospital, but as soon as they are released they will go straight back to the disordered eating behavior again. . . .

Prevention of Eating Disorders

Since treatment for eating disorders is difficult, the best approach is prevention. And successful prevention depends on keeping a healthy self-image and on maintaining a balanced diet.

Maintain a Healthy Self-Image. As we saw earlier, our society's obsession with thinness, together with a constant emphasis on the theme that rich food means pleasure, puts many teens in a bind. Being drawn to excessive eating on the one hand and self-denial on the other can trigger anorexia or bulimia—or both. Anorexics, in particular, seem to feel that no matter how much weight they lose, they are still too fat. When asked to draw themselves, some draw an image of a body much plumper than any mirror or photograph would show them.

Therefore, it is important for each person in our society to try to maintain a healthy and realistic self-image. Don't compare yourself with the models and actors in the media. Set your sights more realistically by comparing yourself with family and friends, if anyone. Better yet, try to find your own strengths and weaknesses without comparing yourself with others at all. In short, don't try to be someone else. Try to be the best person you can uniquely be.

Maintain a Balanced Diet. Prolonged self-denial is the typical first step toward an eating disorder. Eventually,

cravings for what you've denied yourself become unbearable, and you react with either a binge or overly fierce self-control. The answer is not, of course, to indulge in all the snacks and treats you fancy. But to avoid that first step that leads to cravings, strive for a good and healthy diet. Such a diet is based primarily on grain products, fruits, and vegetables, with moderate amounts of meat and dairy products and with small amounts of snacks and desserts. Research demonstrates that this kind of diet leaves you more alert and energetic, with no uncontrollable cravings.

In fact, some research by Stephanie Dalvit-McPhillips found that even among those who have already developed bulimia, this kind of diet can enable them to overcome the tendency to binge. She studied 28 bulimic patients for two and a half years. When chowing down their usual unbalanced diet, they indulged in frequent binges. But when operating on a good diet, they not only stopped the binges completely but even lost weight on the average.

You really can live more happily and healthy with a sound, balanced diet.

1. In paragraph 3, the author writes, "Models in ads . . . and actors in shows . . . are usually physically fit and quite thin." Which of the following positions does this statement support?

   A. Eating disorders should be prevented.
   B. Society encourages people to indulge in food and drink.
   C. Society pressures people to be slim and trim.
   D. Eating a balanced diet promotes healthy living.

2. Which of the following would the author most likely support?

   A. more television shows featuring thin teenagers
   B. greater emphasis by society on self-denial
   C. magazine advertisements that show people enjoying rich foods
   D. school programs that help build a positive self-image

3. The author believes that

   A. the best approach to eating disorders is prevention.
   B. eating disorders are less of a problem than people think.
   C. anorexia is easily cured through hospital treatment.
   D. society is the cause of eating disorders.

4. In this selection, the author is most concerned with

   A. explaining how to make advertisements more realistic.
   B. praising the benefits of psychiatric care.
   C. protecting the well-being of teens and others.
   D. identifying the main cause of eating disorders.

Thinking It Through

1. In paragraph 3, the author writes, "Models in ads . . . and actors in shows . . . are usually physically fit and quite thin." Which of the following positions does this statement support?

    A. Eating disorders should be prevented.

    B. Society encourages people to indulge in food and drink.

    C. Society pressures people to be slim and trim.

    D. Eating a balanced diet promotes healthy living.

    The quoted words come right after, and support, the author's reference to "another dominant pressure in society—to stay slim and trim." The correct answer is choice C. Although the other possible answers are all true, in this context only choice C is directly supported by the quoted statement.

2. Which of the following would the author most likely support?

    A. more television shows featuring thin teenagers

    B. greater emphasis by society on self-denial

    C. magazine advertisements that show people enjoying rich foods

    D. school programs that help build a positive self-image

    This question asks me to make an inference based on my understanding of the author's ideas and point of view. From a careful reading of the selection, I know that the author would not favor the first three choices, but he would certainly support the fourth one. The correct answer is choice D.

3. The author believes that

    A. the best approach to eating disorders is prevention.

    B. eating disorders are less of a problem than people think.

    C. anorexia is easily cured through hospital treatment.

    D. society is the cause of eating disorders.

    I see right away that choice A is correct, but I consider the other possibilities just to be sure. B and C are clearly wrong. Although society may contribute to eating disorders, it's not the sole cause. Therefore, choice D is also wrong.

4. In this selection, the author is most concerned with

    A. explaining how to make advertisements more realistic.

    B. praising the benefits of psychiatric care.

    C. protecting the well-being of teens and others.

    D. identifying the main cause of eating disorders.

This question is asking me to make an inference based on my understanding of the selection and the author's purpose in writing it. The correct answer is choice C. The information and recommendations that the author presents clearly convey his concern for the well-being of people.

TECHNIQUES OF PERSUASION

Much of what you read and hear is persuasive in purpose—words meant to influence how you think or act. *Strong persuasive text is based on solid facts and reasons.* However, when writers and speakers are intent upon convincing you, they may use various techniques to get their message across.

Here are just a few examples of persuasive techniques to watch for. You'll find such techniques in essays, speeches, editorials, advertisements, magazine articles, and most other kinds of text.

- *Unsupported or misleading statements* are meant to convince you without clear or logical reasons. Example: *Since Governor Conlan took office, taxes have increased 10 percent.* (But was it the governor who increased them?)
- *Emotional appeals* try to persuade you by stirring your feelings. Example: *These hungry, homeless families are depending on your generosity. . . .*
- *Propaganda* is distorted or one-sided information meant to influence your opinion. Example: A nation at war may tell its citizens that the enemy is entirely to blame for the conflict.
- *Figurative language* uses words imaginatively to create an effect or an image. Example: *Passing this law would be as foolish as sticking your hand in a fire. You're sure to get burned.*
- *Connotation*, the implied meaning of a word, sends a subtle message. Example: The words *clever*, *sly*, and *shrewd* have similar meanings but different connotations.
- *Repetition* is a means of dramatizing or emphasizing a point. Example: *Julie Chen is an honest woman. Julie Chen is a dedicated woman. Julie Chen is the only woman for the job.*
- *Rhetorical questions* are asked to create an effect or make a point, not to get an answer. Example: *Isn't it about time we put reckless drivers behind bars?*

Activity L: Evaluating Word Choice

You've learned that authors convey their meaning and point of view through their choice of words. In paragraph 9 of "Looking Good, Eating Right," the author refers to "our society's obsession with thinness." Write a paragraph explaining how the author's use of the word *obsession* relates to his purpose and point of view.

_____

_____

_____

_____

_____

_____

_____

_____

_____

_____

REVIEW

Here's a brief summary of what you've learned in section 3.4. To review any of these points in detail, turn to the pages shown.

The basics (pages 94–95):
- → An author's *purpose* is his/her reason or goal for writing.
- → An author's *point of view* is how the author feels about his/her topic or central idea.
- → Purpose and point of view may be stated or implied.
- → Authors achieve their purpose and reveal their point of view through the decisions and choices they make about content, organization, and language.

Understanding an author's purpose and point of view (page 97):
- → Identify the most important ideas in the selection.
- → Consider your reactions to the selection.
- → Think about the author's motive for writing.
- → Think about what's included *and* what's not.
- → Think about how the author organized the content.
- → Notice the author's choice of words.
- → Pay attention to literary elements and writing techniques.

PRACTICE

The activities that follow will give you a chance to practice the strategies that you've learned in this chapter and in Chapter 2. Because HSPA questions call for a combination of skills, some practice questions touch on skills covered in other parts of this book.

Practice Activity 1

Read the selection and answer the questions that follow.

In this newspaper editorial, the writer raises significant issues about a controversial topic.

Justifiable Doubts About the Death Penalty
from *The Star-Ledger*, October 12, 1999

Most New Jerseyans favor the death penalty, convinced, it might seem, that some people must die for what they do.

Except that when pollsters ask, "What if the punishment were life without hope of parole?," the 69 percent for capital punishment drops to 44 percent. That suggests that people do not really want executions. They want appropriate punishment. They want to be safe from the killers.

They are right. It is not the death penalty but life with no parole that offers the best way of achieving those ends. And now that death chambers around the country are active again, the death penalty is beginning to show its flaws, from its inherently unequal application to the grave risk of executing the innocent.

The big flaw is the one any civilized society should find hard to accept, the fact that the law can kill the wrong person with no way to undo that mistake.

New Jersey has yet to execute anyone since reinstatement of the death penalty. But nationally, for every seven people executed, one has been freed.

In some cases, it was because of twists of law and procedure, drunken or incompetent defense attorneys and overzealous prosecutors. That may or may not mean the accused was guilty or not guilty. It does suggest something is wrong with the legal system that is supposed to protect us all.

But the most <u>potent</u> argument against the death penalty is the slew of recent cases that leave no doubt about innocence. People have spent years on death row, and some have come within days of execution, for crimes they did not commit. These cases, rising to double figures in **7**

Illinois alone and more than 80 nationally, involve new evidence, particularly DNA evidence, solid alibis and witnesses who not only <u>recanted</u> but in some instances themselves confessed.

The law has made nearly fatal mistakes, which raises the very possibility that other mistakes may have been buried, **8** and innocence and justice along with them.

Capital punishment does not protect or punish evenly. The race, gender, and income—not only of the defendant but of the victim—all affect how aggressively a case is prosecuted and who ends up on death row.

New Jersey has sent many fewer inmates to death row than other states. But that does not mean we are flawless. **10** A catalog of cases, compiled for the state Supreme Court, showed criminals who committed very similar murders received wildly varying sentences.

Trying to be fair, the law makes a killer's background something that must be considered at sentencing. Usually some awful detail of the defendant's life, from abuse during childhood to drug use at the time of the crime, is what it takes to escape death row. On the other hand, also trying to be fair, the courts permit intensely emotional testimony about what a fine fellow the victim was, which may have the opposite effect.

What <u>ensues</u> is an undignified competition in jury-swaying. Punishment has less to do with the crime than it does **12** with the relative quality of the emotional show the defense or prosecution put on before sentencing.

Whatever people say when they are polled, juries are reluctant to impose the death penalty. They should be.

1. What is the author's purpose in this selection? Be specific.

_____

_____

_____

_____

_____

_____

_____

_____

2. What are the author's main arguments?

_____

_____

_____

_____

_____

_____

_____

_____

_____

3. In paragraph 12, the author refers to a trial as "an undignified competition in jury-swaying" and as an "emotional show." How does this choice of language support the author's position?

_____

_____

_____

_____

_____

_____

_____

_____

4. Did the editorial persuade you? Why or why not?

_____

_____

_____

_____

_____

_____

_____

_____

Practice Activity 2

Review the editorial. Then answer the multiple-choice and open-ended questions below.

1. The word **ensues** as it is used in paragraph 12 means

    A. wins.
    B. causes.
    C. results.
    D. compares.

2. The author believes that juries

    A. do not understand what the death penalty is.
    B. are too reluctant to impose the death penalty.
    C. rarely, if ever, make mistakes.
    D. are too often influenced by emotion.

3. In paragraph 7, the author writes, "People have spent years on death row, and some have come within days of execution for crimes they did not commit." Which of the following positions does this statement support?

    A. Most New Jerseyans are in favor of the death penalty.
    B. Juries are reluctant to apply the death penalty.
    C. New Jersey has sentenced fewer criminals to death row than other states.
    D. The legal system has come close to making fatal errors.

4. Which of the following would the author most likely support?

    A. Faster administration of the death penalty after sentencing.
    B. Life in prison without parole for convicted murderers.
    C. An end to jury trials.
    D. More consistent use of the death penalty from state to state.

5. In paragraph 7, the author refers to "witnesses who not only **recanted** but in some instances themselves confessed." In this context, the word **recanted** means

    A. committed crimes.
    B. repeated their testimony.
    C. left the country.
    D. took back what they had said.

6. In paragraph 8, when the author writes that "other mistakes may have been buried," what does the author mean?

    A. Innocent people may have died.
    B. Witnesses lie when they testify.

    C. Lawyers intentionally hide facts.
    D. Criminals have justly been executed.

7. In paragraph 10, the author writes that "criminals who committed very similar murders received wildly varying sentences." This statement BEST supports which of the following positions?

    A. Capital punishment is not fairly administered.
    B. Too many criminals are sentenced to death.
    C. Emotional testimony should be barred from the courtroom.
    D. Punishment should take into consideration a criminal's background.

8. The word **potent** as it is used in paragraph 7, means

    A. weak.
    B. convincing.
    C. questionable.
    D. specific.

OPEN-ENDED ITEM

9. The title of this editorial is "Justifiable Doubts About the Death Penalty."

    • What ideas and information does the author use to convince you that doubts about the death penalty *are* justified?
    • If use of the death penalty continues, what steps might the author suggest to help protect accused persons?

Use information from the selection to support your response.

3.5 EXAMINING ELEMENTS OF FICTION AND NONFICTION

THE BASICS

As you read in Chapter 2, the Language Arts HSPA contains a narrative selection and a persuasive selection. These selections may come from various sources and may be complete works or excerpts from longer works.

SOURCES OF HSPA SELECTIONS

Nonfiction		Fiction
essays	articles	short stories
editorials	speeches	novels
nonfiction books	letters	

Elements and Techniques of Writing

Every selection you read, whether informational or literary in nature, is a blend of elements. What makes one selection different from another is the unique way in which the author uses and combines these elements.

Some elements of writing are associated mainly with fiction; others, mainly with nonfiction. However, novelists and short story writers commonly use methods of nonfiction, while writers of nonfiction frequently borrow fiction techniques. For example, novelists describe characters and setting in detail, often using figurative language. Magazine writers similarly describe people and places, also using figurative language.

For the HSPA, you should be familiar with a wide range of writing elements and techniques. Study pages 111–113.

Activity M: Examining Elements of Writing

Read the following excerpt, and answer the questions that follow.

> When I first met Daniel, his appearance shocked me. Standing before me was a huge mountain of a man, with tree-limb arms and a bushy black pirate's beard.
>
> "Hello," I began, more than a little intimidated by the scowl on his face. "My name is—"
>
> "I *know* who you are," he growled, cutting me off.
>
> I swallowed hard, not sure that I wanted to continue. The room was dead silent, except for the steady ticking of an unseen clock. I wanted to turn and run out of

that house as fast I could. Had I even suspected what was going to happen that afternoon, I would have.

1. Where do you think this excerpt is from? Give reasons for your choice.

   A. a short story

   B. an essay

   C. a personal narrative

   D. a magazine article

   E. any of the above

   _____

   _____

   _____

   _____

   _____

2. Give two examples of elements of fiction or nonfiction that the writer uses. Be specific.

   _____

   _____

   _____

   _____

FYI   **Narrative Selections Tell a Story**

Narrative writing tells a story. The words *narrative, narration,* and *narrator* all come from a Latin word meaning "tell."

Narrative writing may include historical accounts, biographies, autobiographical essays, and the like. However, the term is more often applied to novels, short stories, fables, and other works of fiction.

STRATEGIES

Use the following strategies to help you understand and analyze the HSPA selections.

➤ **Look beneath the surface.**
Writers—especially writers of fiction and poetry—blend stated and implied ideas. Always look for both. For example, the well-known fable about the tortoise and the hare describes a race between two animals. However, the story has a symbolic meaning beyond the simple plot.

Looking beneath the surface means applying your inference skills to various elements. Consider setting and mood, for example. Suppose that a writer begins a selection by describing a small town that has old, run-down buildings and few inhabitants. Such a setting suggests an ill-fated town and sets a dark mood for the selection.

To review strategies for making inferences, refer to section 3.2, "Making Inferences and Drawing Conclusions" (pages 62–63).

➢ **For fiction, think about characters and plot.**
Authors of fiction convey their ideas, feelings, and values through the characters and plot they create. Nothing in a story just "happens." The author *makes* everything happen, and he/she does so for a reason. As you read, try to figure out what that reason is by asking yourself questions such as the following.

ABOUT CHARACTERS:

How does the author feel about this character?
Why does this character act as he/she does?
What is the purpose of this dialogue?

ABOUT PLOT:

What is the author suggesting with this plot development?
What is the purpose of this scene?
Why does the author end the story this way?

➢ **Pay attention to structure.**
How does the author organize his/her content? Does he/she begin with the most recent events or describe events in the order they happened? Does the author use facts and details to build to a conclusion? The answers to such questions will help you understand the author's purpose and central idea.

To read about methods of organization, refer to the box on page 51 and also to "Patterns of Development," on pages 70–72.

➢ **Consider the blend of elements.**
To fully appreciate an author's work, note how its "pieces" work together to form a whole. For example, writers of satire often combine irony and hyperbole to poke fun at people or ideas.

➢ **Think about the writer's use of language.**
Authors of both fiction and nonfiction use figures of speech, imagery, repetition, and other elements and techniques to communicate ideas and feelings. Read with care to understand the full meaning of an author's words.

ELEMENTS AND TECHNIQUES OF FICTION, NONFICTION, AND POETRY

Allegory is the representation of ideas or moral principles through symbolic characters, events, or objects. For example, Aesop's fables use allegory to teach lessons about life.

Alliteration is the repetition of an initial (usually consonant) sound, as in *swift, silent serpent.*

Characterization refers to the creation and development of **characters,** the people who carry on the action in a literary work.

Dialogue refers to the spoken conversation of fictional characters or real people.

Figurative language refers to the use of words in an imaginative, non-literal sense. Similes and metaphors (see below) are examples of figurative language.

Figures of speech are forms of expression in which the author uses language in an imaginative, non-literal sense to make a comparison or produce a desired effect. Common figures of speech include the following:

> A **simile** is a comparison using *like* or *as.* Examples: *His eyes gleamed like stars. The house was as large as a castle.*
>
> A **metaphor** is an implied comparison that does not use *like* or *as.* Example: *They were tigers on the playing field, ferociously mauling their opponents.*
>
> **Personification** is the giving of human qualities to objects, ideas, or animals. Example: *The sun smiled down on the village.*
>
> **Hyperbole,** or **exaggeration,** is overstatement for the purpose of emphasis. Example: *Her ears were so sharp she could hear dogs bark in the next county.*
>
> **Onomatopoeia** refers to the use of words that sound like the things they name. Examples: *bang, buzz, crackle, sizzle, hiss, murmur, roar*
>
> An **oxymoron** is a combination of two contradictory words. Examples: *deafening silence; a definite possibility*

Flashback refers to the insertion of a scene that shows an earlier event, often one that happened before the opening scene of a literary work. For example, a novelist may include a flashback to show an event that happened during the childhood of an adult character.

Foreshadowing refers to the suggestion of events to come. For example, gray clouds at the beginning of a story may foreshadow a storm that occurs later.

Imagery refers to the use of description or figurative language. Authors create vivid **images,** or word pictures, through their creative use of language. These images may appeal to the sense of sight or to any of the other senses. Examples: *Thick tree roots clutched the ground like gnarled fingers. The screech of an animal shattered the night silence.*

Irony refers to a situation or event that is the opposite of what is or might be expected. For example, it would be *ironic* if a lifeguard had to be saved from drowning.

Irony can also refer to the expression of an attitude or intention that is the opposite of what is actually meant, as when a latecomer is sarcastically told, "We're so glad you could join us!"

Mood refers to the atmosphere or feeling of a work. For example, the mood of a selection may be joyful, gloomy, or suspenseful.

The **plot** of a short story, novel, or other literary work is the sequence of events that take place.

Point of view has more than one meaning, depending on the context.

Point of view may refer to how a story is told. For example, in *first-person* point of view, the narrator himself or herself tells the story and may participate in events. Works written in the first person use pronouns such as *I*, *me*, and *my*. In *omniscient* (all-knowing) point of view, the author is an impersonal observer who does not take part in events. Works written in omniscient point of view are written in the third person and use pronouns such as *he, she, his,* and *hers.* Authors using omniscient point of view can describe the thoughts and actions of all characters.

Point of view can also refer to how an author feels about his/her topic or central idea. To review this meaning of the term, see section 3.4, "Understanding an Author's Purpose and Point of View."

Repetition is the repeating of a word or group of words for effect. For example, Archibald MacLeish's poem "The End of the World" ends with these lines:

There in the sudden blackness the black pall
Of nothing, nothing, nothing—nothing at all.

A **rhetorical question** is a question asked only for effect or to make a statement, not to get an answer. Example: *How much longer will we put up with this injustice? Isn't it time that we took action?*

Satire refers to writing that uses humor, irony, or wit to attack or make fun of something, such as people's follies or vices.

Setting is the time and place in which events occur. For example, the setting of Shakespeare's play *Macbeth* is eleventh-century Scotland.

Structure refers to how the parts of a work are organized and arranged. For example, the structure of a novel or biography may be based on chronological (time) order with occasional *flashbacks* (see above). The structure of poetry includes the number, form, and pattern of lines and stanzas.

Symbolism is the representation of ideas or things by symbols. A **symbol** is something that stands for something else. For example, an author may use a rose as a symbol of beauty or a snake as a symbol of evil.

The **theme** (or **central idea**) is the principal point of a work, the main focus or underlying meaning. For example, many authors have written on the theme that life is short, so everyone must make the most of each day. To review this term in detail, see section 3.1, "Identifying Important Ideas and Information."

Tone is the attitude or viewpoint that an author shows toward his/her subject. For example, tone may be serious, sympathetic, optimistic, or angry.

Activity N: Exploring Plot Development

Here is part of the plot of a short story.

Cathy is one of the most obnoxious students at Williams High School. Her rudeness and superior attitude has earned her far more enemies than friends.

Yesterday, a teacher's laptop computer was stolen at school. This morning it was found in Cathy's locker. Cathy denies any knowledge of the theft, but the evidence seems to speak for itself.

However, Isaac saw another student carrying the laptop late yesterday afternoon. The student, a shy boy named Tim, was rushing down the hallway toward the lockers. Isaac knows that Tim has a grudge against Cathy because she embarrassed him in front of a girl he likes.

1. Suppose you are the author of this short story. Briefly describe how you would develop the plot and end the story.

   _____

   _____

   _____

   _____

   _____

2. Based on the same partial plot above, briefly describe an entirely *different* way in which you could develop the plot and end the story.

   _____

   _____

   _____

   _____

3. Compare the two possible plots that you described. How would differences in characters, story development, and final outcome send a different message to readers?

   _____

   _____

   _____

   _____

   _____

   _____

   _____

   _____

APPLYING YOUR KNOWLEDGE

1. Read the selection and answer the questions. Use the strategies that you've learned in this chapter *and* in Chapter 2.

2. After you've finished, read "Thinking It Through" to see how one student answered the questions.

Life's events can sometimes cause deep pain, but as this story shows, they can also bring unexpected healing.

"You're Not My Son!"
by Betty Kjelgaard

The boy entered their lives one June evening, against Jim Talbert's will. Barbara Talbert had answered the ringing telephone and come out to the porch where Jim sat, the two Irish setters behind his chair.

It had been Clayt McConnell, the county commissioner, she'd said. The county had had to take over five children whose parents had deserted them. Clayt had them all farmed out to responsible people except the oldest. Would the Talberts take him for a couple of months? They had this big place outside of town, and Jim had been saying at the last Lions' Club meeting that he needed help with the lawn and the shrubs. . . .

"How old is he?" Jim asked.

"Almost sixteen," Barbara said. The blur of her face was turned toward him in the twilight. She was very still.

He looked straight ahead at the mountains. "What did you tell Clayt?" But he had the feeling he already knew.

"I told him—" her voice faltered, then steadied—"I told him we did need someone. Clayt's bringing him out tonight."

Well, she's half the household, Jim thought. *She's got a right to state her wants, too.*

Quietly, Barbara said, "You can't stay in a cave forever because we lost Rusty."

That's what everybody said. That's why Clayt had saved this boy for them. Well-intentioned people could be cruel; and you were helpless against that kind of cruelty. "If that's it, then," he said, "why, that's it."

So he had been prepared for the boy's arrival half an hour later. But he was not prepared for the terrible identity that leaped in him when the boy got out of the car and walked toward the porch. After a year and a half of avoiding the school and the football field and any place where boys might hang out, he had to sit there and watch one approach with that awkward grace of all teen-agers who have grown too tall too fast. Clayt introduced him as Richard Dodd, better known as Tick. His face was indistinct in the deepening night, but he was plainly very uncomfortable until one of the watchful setters moved behind the chair. His quick eyes saw them both then, and he dropped down on his heels, all uneasiness gone.

"Oh, golly," he breathed, "oh, golly."

That was Rusty, too. Jim turned away so harshly that an ash tray went clattering to the floor. "I've got work to do," he said. "See you, Clayt."

Out of the silence behind him, Barbara's voice came, bright. "This is Lady and this is Reb," she said. "They're hunting dogs, Tick."

When Jim went into the kitchen the next morning, Tick was sitting at the table and Barbara was fixing bacon and eggs.

"Good morning, Mr. Talbert," Tick said, in a quiet way.

"Good morning," Jim said politely. He let his glance flicker over the boy. Brown hair he saw, blue eyes too big for that thin face, a good chin.

"What would you like me to do today, sir?" Tick said.

Jim turned to Barbara. "What would you like him to do today?"

Her look met his. She understood. He was denying any association between himself and Tick. "I thought we might work in the rock garden," she said. Her voice was level.

"Fine."

A little later, driving to his insurance office in town, Jim decided he had set the best possible course. He had no grudge against the boy. It was just that he couldn't be expected to lavish love on every waif who stumbled along. He had no love to give, actually. Rusty, his only son and child, had gone with dreadful swiftness, dying in the bud without ever having a chance to unfold. Because he seemed to have merely a mild sore throat, Jim had not been alarmed. Then meningitis struck, sweeping Rusty out before anyone could help. Though he was blameless, Jim in his mind had said over and over, *If only I had known, or been more alert.* By that time it was too late, and so his spirit was imprisoned when his son left him. But boys had a way of resembling each other, and for that reason you had to build up a defense. If you didn't, memories could be stabbing all the time.

Tick had done a good job on the rock garden. He did a good job on the lawn, too, and on the shrubs. He ran errands for Barbara, helped her with the dishes and the housework. And spent all his free time with the setters. Jim was driving in one August afternoon when Tick came loping around the corner of the garage with Lady and Reb. He stopped short when he saw Jim.

Jim got out and fondled the leaping dogs, noting the super-brilliance of the dark red coats. "You brushed 'em?" he asked Tick.

"Yes, sir." The boy hesitated, then said, "They're great hunters, Mr. Talbert! We were in the woods and two grouse flew up and—"

"That's what they're trained for, Tick," Jim said shortly, and walked away. The boy's rare eagerness had broken through his precious guard for a moment, so that he had had a flashing picture of himself teaching Rusty to hunt behind the dogs. The cheerful insults would have flown back and forth across the brush, that special language of father and son; and always the bridge of closeness would have been there, warm, binding. . . .

Barbara was in the kitchen. She kissed him and said, "I was watching you and Tick. If you could have seen the way he brushed those dogs today!" She laughed. "He keeps whispering to them, like someone with a deep secret."

"Yeah," Jim said. He had seen that too, the soft absent look on Tick's face. "Saturday Doc Egan and Sam Hawke are coming out with their pups and we're going to start getting them and Lady and Reb in shape for hunting season."

Her eyes searched him skillfully. Then she moved toward the cupboard, saying over her shoulder, "Do you want iced coffee or iced tea for dinner?"

"Coffee," he said, puzzled, and went on up the stairs.

At five o'clock Saturday morning he waited for Doc and Sam to arrive. Because the leashed dogs were impatient, he walked them into the field across the road. Coming back, he could see his house, clean and pleasant in the dawn. His look climbed up Rusty's room and clung there until a flicker at another window made his glance swerve. That was the room Tick had. Jim frowned. Was Tick standing behind the curtain? Everything was still as still.

Then Doc Egan's station wagon came into view and Jim went to meet it. It was nothing, he thought, just wishful thinking—a desire to see a boy I'll never see again except in mind and heart.

They worked the dogs until the thick heat of midday drove them home. But they went again the following Saturday. The next Friday Jim was sitting on the porch before dinner when Barbara appeared.

"Are you going to take the dogs out tomorrow?" she asked.

"Doc and Sam can't make it," Jim said, "but I thought I would."

Barbara said, "Will you take Tick along?"

No, something inside him said instantly, *almost anything but that*. "Why?" he asked.

"Well, not only because he would love to go," Barbara said, "but because Clayt McConnell was here today. School starts week after next, and Tick has one more year. Clayt said if we weren't going to—keep him, there's a farmer out at Dry Run who'll give him room and board in exchange for Tick's helping with the chores. That means he'll be leaving us in a few days."

"Would it mean a lot to you if I took Tick tomorrow?" he said.

"Yes," she said evenly.

He put on a smile for her. "O.K."

Tick was in the kitchen when Jim got down the next morning.

"I've got breakfast nearly ready, Mr. Talbert," he said.

"So I see," Jim said. "I didn't hear your alarm go off."

"It didn't," Tick said, almost shyly. "I was awake."

Jim poured coffee with steady hands, thinking of how Rusty would come in and nudge him at four-thirty, his eyes aglow, as he whispered, "Hey, time's awasting; get up!"

They ate in silence that was not painful because they were both used to it. Then they piled the dogs in the car and drove away.

"Now keep me in sight," Jim instructed, "so you can get my signals. The dogs will range afield. When they come to a full point, be careful. Move very slowly and very quietly. I'll break the point by shooting my pistol. Do you understand?"

"Yes, sir," Tick said.

25

Jim parked at the edge of a field which was full of old corn shocks and stubble. Ahead was a thicket. Tick's thin shoulders were trembling a little. Jim told him to wait, walked fifty yards to the left, loosed the dogs, and motioned Tick forward. They followed the setters across the field and into the thicket until Jim saw Lady alert herself in the familiar way that told him she had sighted birds.

He glanced across at Tick, intending to signal caution because the dog would close in for the point. But the boy was watching Lady with fascinated eyes and walking forward eagerly. Jim felt a jar, as if a chink had come open. That was Rusty's trouble too, he thought: jumping the gun. His heart began to pound then, and suddenly it was another day in another year and a brown-haired boy was there and everything was allright with the world. Something long-controlled let loose in Jim, pouring out in a joyous gush.

51 "You lop-eared, blockheaded, lollapaloozing young ape!" he yelled. "I told you to hold up when the dogs began to point!"

And back came a boy's happy laughter. "O.K., Dad!"

Complete silence fell. They stared at each other. Tick licked his lips and swallowed. He said that, Jim thought, as if he'd been thinking it for a long time. O.K., Dad! The words filled him and released him from the past to a future. Get a little more meat on his bones, he thought, and he'll start growing up to his eyes. We'll see to that, Barbara and I. **53**

"You'll learn," he called to Tick, his voice not quite steady. "Let's try it again."

"O.K.—" Tick called back, and shut his mouth.

He almost said it again, Jim thought. He grinned at Tick and shyly the boy grinned back. The bridge of closeness was beginning between them, warm, binding. . . .

1. In paragraph 21, the author writes that Rusty died "in the bud without ever having a chance to unfold." This is an example of

   A. metaphor.
   B. simile.
   C. personification.
   D. hyperbole.

2. In paragraph 12, "Jim turned away so harshly that an ash tray went clattering to the floor." This sentence suggests that

   A. Jim is a large man.
   B. Jim is upset because Tick reminds him of Rusty.
   C. Jim has taken an instant dislike to Tick.
   D. Jim thinks boys like Rusty and Tick spend too much time playing with dogs.

3. Which of the following is an example of a metaphor, a literary device used in the story?

   A. "Clayt introduced him as Richard Dodd, better known as Tick."
   B. "The boy entered their lives one June evening, against Jim Talbert's will."

   C. "'He keeps whispering to them, like someone with a deep secret.'"
   D. "'You can't stay in a cave forever because we lost Rusty.'"

4. What does the sentence, "The words filled him and released him from the past to a future" in paragraph 53 suggest?

   A. Jim will no longer think about Rusty.
   B. Jim is ready to open his heart to another boy.
   C. Jim has never liked being referred to as "Dad."
   D. Jim plans to have many more children.

5. In paragraph 51, Jim yells at Tick that he's a "lop-eared, blockheaded, lollapaloozing young ape." Jim's words most likely show that he

   A. does not like Tick.
   B. will never again go hunting with Tick.
   C. has begun to accept Tick.
   D. is furious at Tick's bad judgment.

6. In paragraph 25, the author refers to the "bridge of closeness . . . warm, binding. . . ." In the last paragraph of the story, the author uses these same words again. This is an example of

    A. irony.
    B. foreshadowing.
    C. repetition for effect.
    D. alliteration.

7. At the end of the story, Jim thinks, "We'll see to that, Barbara and I" (paragraph 54). This sentence implies that

    A. the Talberts will help Clayt McConnell find a good home for Tick.
    B. Tick will have a fine dinner at the Talberts' home that night.

    C. Tick will be well cared for living with the farmer at Dry Run.
    D. Tick will remain with the Talberts.

8. Throughout the story, Barbara's words and actions suggest that she

    A. understands her husband's feelings but welcomes Tick.
    B. loved Rusty more than her husband did.
    C. prefers Tick to Rusty.
    D. thinks her husband is behaving in an unreasonable way.

Thinking It Through

1. In paragraph 21, the author writes that Rusty died "in the bud without ever having a chance to unfold." This is an example of

    A. metaphor.
    B. simile.
    C. personification.
    D. hyperbole.

    In the quoted lines, the author is comparing Rusty to a flower that died before it ever could open. I recognize this as a metaphor—an implied comparison that does not use the word like or as. The correct answer is choice A.

2. In paragraph 12, "Jim turned away so harshly that an ash tray went clattering to the floor." This sentence suggests that

    A. Jim is a large man.
    B. Jim is upset because Tick reminds him of Rusty.
    C. Jim has taken an instant dislike to Tick.
    D. Jim thinks boys like Rusty and Tick spend too much time playing with dogs.

    To answer this question, I have to carefully reread and think about the context, especially paragraph 12 . I notice that just before Jim turns, he sees Tick's reaction to the dogs and automatically compares him with Rusty ("That was Rusty, too"). I think this sudden remembrance jars Jim and causes him to move away, to distance himself. Based on my inference, I pick choice B as the correct answer.

3. Which of the following is an example of a metaphor, a literary device used in the story?

    A. "Clayt introduced him as Richard Dodd, better known as Tick."
    B. "The boy entered their lives one June evening, against Jim Talbert's will."
    C. "'He keeps whispering to them, like someone with a deep secret.'"
    D. "'You can't stay in a cave forever because we lost Rusty.'"

I do not see a literary device in choices A or B. Choice C contains a simile: he whispers like someone with a secret. In choice D, Jim is compared to someone hiding in a cave. This is an implied comparison that doesn't use like or as. The correct answer is choice D.

4. What does the sentence, "The words filled him and released him from the past to a future" in paragraph 53 suggest?

    A. Jim will no longer think about Rusty.
    B. Jim is ready to open his heart to another boy.
    C. Jim has never liked being referred to as "Dad."
    D. Jim plans to have many more children.

This question asks me to make an inference based on the plot and on my understanding of the character Jim. I think that choice B is the correct answer. The interaction between Jim and Tick at the end of the story suggests that Jim is finally ready to move on from the past to the future. None of the other choices is supported by the text.

5. In paragraph 51, Jim yells at Tick that he's a "lop-eared, blockheaded, lollapaloozing young ape." Jim's words most likely show that he

    A. does not like Tick.
    B. will never again go hunting with Tick.
    C. has begun to accept Tick.
    D. is furious at Tick's bad judgment.

I think choice C is the correct answer. Earlier in the story (paragraph 25), the author describes the "cheerful insults" that were part of the special relationship between father and son when they went hunting together. I don't think Jim is really angry or upset—and neither does Tick, since he responds with "happy laughter."

6. In paragraph 25, the author refers to the "bridge of closeness . . . warm, binding. . . ." In the last paragraph of the story, the author uses these same words again. This is an example of

    A. irony.
    B. foreshadowing.
    C. repetition for effect.
    D. alliteration.

The "bridge of closeness" is mentioned twice, once with regard to Rusty, the second time referring to Tick. This repetition is for effect. The author is showing that Jim has finally let down his guard, allowing a relationship to begin between him and Tick. The correct answer is choice C.

7. At the end of the story, Jim thinks, "We'll see to that, Barbara and I" (paragraph 54). This sentence implies that

   A.   the Talberts will help Clayt McConnell find a good home for Tick.
   B.   Tick will have a fine dinner at the Talberts' home that night.
   C.   Tick will be well cared for living with the farmer at Dry Run.
   D.   Tick will remain with the Talberts.

By the end of the story, Jim has started to feel something for Tick. Since Barbara also appears to like Tick, I can conclude that they will want him to stay with them. The correct answer is choice D.

8. Throughout the story, Barbara's words and actions suggest that she

   A.   understands her husband's feelings but welcomes Tick.
   B.   loved Rusty more than her husband did.
   C.   prefers Tick to Rusty.
   D.   thinks her husband is behaving in an unreasonable way.

From the very beginning, Barbara is a low-key but clearly positive influence. She is supportive and understanding toward Jim, but also does what she can to help her husband accept Tick's presence. For example, she reminds Jim that he "can't stay in a cave forever because we lost Rusty." Choice A is the correct answer.

Activity O: Writing a Response to a Story

A.   Plan and write a response for the following open-ended item.

In "You're Not My Son!" the arrival of Tick in the Talberts' home has a significant effect on the main characters.

   •   How do Jim Talbert's feelings change during the story?
   •   How will the story's conclusion affect the lives of Jim, Barbara, and Tick?

Use information from the story to support your response.

_____

_____

_____

_____

_____

_____

_____

_____

_____

_____

_____

_____

_____

_____

_____

B. **Peer feedback**. Work with a partner. Exchange the responses you wrote, and evaluate each other's work on the basis of the following questions. Make constructive and specific comments.

   - Did the student understand the selection?
   - Did the student understand the questions and the writing task?
   - How clearly and effectively did the student answer the questions?
   - How much insight into the selection and the questions did the student's answer show?
   - Did the student adequately support his/her answer with ideas and details from the selection?

REVIEW

Here's a brief summary of what you've learned in section 3.5. To review any of these points in detail, turn to the pages shown.

The basics (pages 108–109):

→   Every selection is a combination of elements. What makes each selection unique is how the writer uses and blends these elements.

→   Some elements and techniques of writing are associated mainly with fiction. Others are associated mainly with nonfiction. However, there are no "rules." Fiction writers use nonfiction methods, and writers of nonfiction use fiction techniques.

Examining elements of fiction and nonfiction (pages 109–110):

→   Look beneath the surface.

→   For fiction, think about characters and plot.

→   Pay attention to structure.

→   Consider the blend of elements.

→   Think about the writer's use of language.

PRACTICE

The activities that follow will give you a chance to practice the strategies that you've learned in this chapter and in Chapter 2. Because HSPA questions call for a combination of skills, some practice questions touch on skills covered in other parts of this book.

Practice Activity 1

Read the selection and answer the multiple-choice and open-ended questions that follow.

Reminder: Use the strategies that you learned in this chapter *and* in Chapter 2.

A brief encounter can affect a person's life. The following story explores this idea through the experience of two characters.

Thank You, M'am
by Langston Hughes

She was a large woman with a large purse that had everything in it but a hammer and nails. It had a long strap, and she carried it slung across her shoulder. It was about eleven o'clock at night, dark, and she was walking alone, when a boy ran up behind her and tried to snatch her purse. The strap broke with the sudden single tug the boy gave it from behind. But the boy's weight and the weight of the purse combined caused him to lose his balance. Instead of taking off full blast as he had hoped, the boy fell on his back on the sidewalk and his legs flew up. The large woman simply turned around and kicked him right square in his blue-jeaned sitter. Then she reached down, picked the boy up by his shirt front, and shook him until his teeth rattled.

After that the woman said, "Pick up my pocketbook, boy, and give it here."

She still held him tightly. But she bent down enough to permit him to stoop and pick up her purse. Then she said, "Now ain't you ashamed of yourself?"

Firmly gripped by his shirt front, the boy said, "Yes'm."

The woman said, "What did you want to do it for?"

The boy said, "I didn't aim to."

She said, "You a lie!"

By that time two or three people passed, stopped, turned to look, and some stood watching.

"If I turn you loose, will you run?" asked the woman.

"Yes'm," said the boy.

"Then I won't turn you loose," said the woman. She did not release him.

"Lady, I'm sorry," whispered the boy.

"Um-hum! Your face is dirty. I got a great mind to wash your face for you. Ain't you got nobody home to tell you to wash your face?"

"No'm," said the boy.

"Then it will get washed this evening," said the large woman, starting up the street, dragging the frightened boy behind her.

He looked as if he were fourteen or fifteen, frail and willow-wild, in tennis shoes and blue jeans.

The woman said, "You ought to be my son. I would teach you right from wrong. Least I can do right now is to wash your face. Are you hungry?"

"No'm," said the being-dragged boy. "I just want you to turn me loose."

"Was I bothering *you* when I turned that corner?" asked the woman.

"No'm."

"But you put yourself in contact with *me*," said the woman. "If you think that that contact is not going to last awhile, you got another thought coming. When I get through with you, sir, you are going to remember Mrs. Luella Bates Washington Jones."

Sweat popped out on the boy's face and he began to struggle. Mrs. Jones stopped, jerked him around in front of her, put a half nelson about his neck, and continued to drag him up the street. When she got to her door, she dragged the boy inside, down a hall, and into a large kitchenette-furnished room at the rear of the house. She switched on the light and left the door open. The boy could hear other roomers laughing and talking in the large house. Some of their doors were open, too, so he knew he and the woman were not alone. The woman still had him by the neck in the middle of her room.

She said, "What is your name?"

"Roger," answered the boy.

"Then, Roger, you go to that sink and wash your face," said the woman, whereupon she turned him loose—at last. Roger looked at the door—looked at the woman—looked at the door—*and went to the sink.*

"Let the water run until it gets warm," she said. "Here's a clean towel."

"You gonna take me to jail?" asked the boy, bending over the sink.

"Not with that face, I would not take you nowhere," said the woman. "Here I am trying to get home to cook me a bite to eat, and you snatch my pocketbook! Maybe you ain't been to your supper either, late as it be. Have you?"

"There's nobody home at my house," said the boy.

"Then we'll eat," said the woman. "I believe you're hungry—or been hungry—to try to snatch my pocketbook!"

"I want a pair of blue suede shoes," said the boy.

"Well, you didn't have to snatch *my* pocketbook to get some suede shoes," said Mrs. Luella Bates Washington Jones. "You could of asked me."

"M'am?"

The water dripping from his face, the boy looked at her. There was a long pause. A very long pause. After he had dried his face and, not knowing what else to do, dried it again, the boy turned around, wondering what next. The door was open. He could make a dash for it down the hall. He could run, run, run, *run!*

35 The woman was sitting on the day bed. After a while she said, "I were young once and I wanted things I could not get."

There was another long pause. The boy's mouth opened. Then he frowned, not knowing he frowned.

The woman said, "Uh-hum! You thought I was going to say *but,* didn't you? You thought I was going to say, *but I didn't snatch people's pocketbooks.* Well, I wasn't going

to say that." Pause. Silence. "I have done things, too, which I would not tell you, son—neither tell God, if He didn't already know. Everybody's got something in common. So you set down while I fix us something to eat. You might run that comb through your hair so you will look presentable."

In another corner of the room behind a screen was a gas plate and an icebox. Mrs. Jones got up and went behind the screen. The woman did not watch the boy to see if he was going to run now, nor did she watch her purse, which she left behind her on the day bed. But the boy took care **38** to sit on the far side of the room, away from the purse, where he thought she could easily see him out of the corner of her eye if she wanted to. He did not trust the woman *not* to trust him. And he did not want to be mistrusted now.

"Do you need somebody to go to the store," asked the boy, "maybe to get some milk or something?"

"Don't believe I do," said the woman, "unless you just want sweet milk yourself. I was going to make cocoa out of this canned milk I got here."

"That will be fine," said the boy.

She heated some lima beans and ham she had in the icebox, made the cocoa, and set the table. The woman did not ask the boy anything about where he lived, or his folks, or anything else that would embarrass him. Instead, as they ate, she told him about her job in a hotel beauty shop that stayed open late, what the work was like, and how all kinds of women came in and out, blondes, redheads, and Spanish. Then she cut him a half of her ten-cent cake.

"Eat some more, son," she said.

When they were finished eating, she got up and said, "Now here, take this ten dollars and buy yourself some blue suede shoes. And next time, do not make the mistake of <u>latching onto</u> *my* pocketbook *nor nobody else's*—be- **44** cause shoes got by devilish ways will burn your feet. I got to get my rest now. But from here on in, son, I hope you will behave yourself."

She led him down the hall to the front door and opened it. "Good night! Behave yourself, boy!" she said, looking out into the street as he went down the steps.

The boy wanted to say something other than, "Thank you, m'am," to Mrs. Luella Bates Washington Jones, but although his lips moved, he couldn't even say that as he turned at the foot of the barren stoop and looked up at the large woman in the door. Then she shut the door.

1. The story begins with the sentence: "She was a large woman with a large purse that had everything in it but a hammer and nails." This is an example of

   A. onomatopoeia.
   B. personification.
   C. metaphor.
   D. hyperbole.

2. Mrs. Jones tells the boy not to "make the mistake of **latching onto** *my* pocketbook *nor nobody else's*" (paragraph 44). In this context, **latching onto** means

   A. grabbing.
   B. admiring.
   C. closing.
   D. opening.

3. The boy and Mrs. Jones meet because

   A. Mrs. Jones was looking for a helper.
   B. the boy intended to rob her.
   C. Mrs. Jones wanted to help the boy.
   D. the boy wanted to help Mrs. Jones.

4. Mrs. Jones takes the boy to her home because

   A. she wants to encourage him to keep out of trouble.
   B. she needs someone to go to the store for her.
   C. the boy asks to come along.
   D. she wants a dinner companion.

5. As the story unfolds, the boy's feelings change from

   A. fear to gratitude to bitterness.
   B. gratitude to curiosity to resentment.
   C. fear to bewilderment to gratitude.
   D. calmness to anger to fear.

6. Mrs. Jones' actions and words suggest that she

   A. is a wealthy person.
   B. hopes to form a close friendship with the boy.
   C. expects the boy to repay her.
   D. sympathizes with the boy's situation.

7. Which of the following BEST expresses the theme of the story?

   A. Honesty is the best policy.
   B. An act of kindness may change someone's life.
   C. Being poor may lead a person to a life of crime.
   D. People should not interfere in the lives of others.

8. In paragraph 35, Mrs. Jones tells the boy, "I were young once and I wanted things I could not get." This statement suggests that Mrs. Jones

   A. thinks that she is smarter than the boy.
   B. wanted a pair of blue suede shoes when she was a teenager.
   C. thinks that she and the boy have something in common.
   D. has learned that some things are not worth having.

OPEN-ENDED ITEM

9. Before taking him to her home, the woman tells the boy, "When I get through with you, sir, you are going to remember Mrs. Luella Bates Washington Jones."

   • What is it that Mrs. Jones hopes to accomplish?
   • How may the boy benefit from his experience with Mrs. Jones?

   Use information from the selection to support your response.

_____

_____

_____

_____

_____

_____

_____

_____

_____

_____

_____

_____

_____

_____

Practice Activity 2

Answer the following questions about "Thank You M'am."

1. In paragraph 38, the author writes: "He did not trust the woman *not* to trust him. And he did not want to be mistrusted now." Explain why these two sentences are significant.

_____

_____

_____

_____

_____

_____

_____

_____

_____

2. What kind of life has Mrs. Jones led, as a young person and as an adult? Use specific information from the story to support your answer.

_____

_____

_____

_____

_____

_____

_____

_____

_____

C H A P T E R   4

HSPA WRITING TASKS

As you've seen, the Language Arts HSPA asks you to write responses to open-ended questions about reading selections. In addition, the exam has three other writing tasks that differ from the open-ended questions:

- writing about a picture
- writing a persuasive essay or letter
- revising and editing a given essay

For each of these tasks, you'll respond to some kind of prompt. A *prompt* consists of directions and information explaining exactly what you have to do for part of a test.

For instance, one HSPA prompt guides your response to a picture, while another describes the persuasive essay or letter you'll write. In this chapter, you'll see examples of the different kinds of writing prompts that appear on the HSPA.

The guidelines presented in this chapter will help you do your best on the tasks highlighted below.

☑ **HSPA READING AND WRITING TASKS**

✔	**Part 1:**	Write an extended response about a picture.
	Part 2:	Read a persuasive selection and answer multiple-choice and open-ended questions.
✔	**Part 3:**	Revise and edit a given student essay.
	Part 4:	Read a narrative selection and answer multiple-choice and open-ended questions.
✔	**Part 5:**	Write a persuasive essay or letter.

SCORING STANDARDS FOR EXTENDED RESPONSES

Because the HSPA writing tasks differ from one another, they are not all scored in the same way. However, the extended responses that you write for Parts 1 and 5 are scored on the basis of the same standards. These standards are summarized in the chart below.

SCORING STANDARDS FOR EXTENDED RESPONSES

Content and Organization
- ✓ Gets meaning across to intended audience
- ✓ Has an opening and a closing
- ✓ Clear, single focus
- ✓ Unity
- ✓ Coherence
- ✓ Well-developed ideas
- ✓ Effective use of details

Usage
- ✓ Few errors in tense, agreement, word choice, and the like

Sentence Construction
- ✓ Variety in structure and length of sentences
- ✓ Few errors

Mechanics
- ✓ Few errors in spelling, capitalization, or punctuation

The meaning of *Usage*, *Sentence Construction*, and *Mechanics* in the chart is probably clear to you. However, let's take a closer look at the items listed under *Content and Organization*.

Content and Organization

As the chart suggests, content and organization work together. *Content* is the substance of your writing—your ideas and supporting information. *Organization* is the structure that gives your content shape and direction. To review methods of organization and development, see the boxed features on page 51 ("Methods of Organization") and pages 70–72 ("Patterns of Development").

The responses you write for the HSPA should be clearly focused on your topic. Your main ideas should be well developed with specific and relevant supporting information.

To learn more about the organization of extended responses, study the box below.

STRUCTURE OF EXTENDED RESPONSES

Written responses vary widely but generally should have these elements:

OPENING
Introduces the topic and the central idea

BODY
Supports and develops the central idea

CLOSING
Summarizes or reinforces the most important ideas or otherwise brings the composition to conclusion

- Depending on the kind of writing task and the length of your response, the opening and closing may or may not be separate paragraphs.
- The *central idea* is the principal point, the main focus or underlying meaning. The central idea is like a thread tying together all the paragraphs. The central idea is also called the *theme, thesis,* or *controlling idea.*
- The central idea may be stated or implied. In persuasive and informational text, writers usually state their central idea directly. In narrative text, writers more commonly imply their point through events and characters.
- The sentence that states a thesis (central idea) is the *thesis statement.* In general, essays and other long responses include a thesis statement in the first paragraph to establish the focus. (Shorter responses can establish their focus with topic sentences.) Thesis statements should be clear and specific.
- The body paragraphs work together to develop the central idea. The *main idea* of each paragraph is the idea that holds the paragraph together. It's what the whole paragraph is about.

Your writing should have both unity and coherence. To have *unity*, an essay or other written response must communicate a clear central idea, and every paragraph must relate to that idea. This means leaving out ideas and information that are not relevant to the topic.

Coherence comes from a Latin word meaning "stick together." For writing to be coherent, your ideas must "stick together." That is, you have to blend them into a smoothly flowing whole.

You can use *transitional words and phrases* to connect ideas and details and help readers follow your organizational structure. For examples of transitional words and phrases, study the box on pages 132–133.

UNITY AND COHERENCE

Unified writing

➡ **Communicates a clear central idea**

➡ **Every paragraph relates to that idea**

Coherent writing

➡ **Clearly and logically organized**
Flows in a way that makes sense and is easy for readers to follow

➡ **Stays focused**
Has a clear topic and sticks to it

➡ **Smoothly connected**
Uses transitional words and phrases to connect ideas

Activity A: Understanding the Scoring Standards

Read an essay in a book or magazine. (Your teacher may assign an essay to the class.) Then use the questions below to evaluate the essay. The questions are based on the "Scoring Standards for Extended Responses" (page 128).

For each question, rate the essay on a scale of 1 to 6, with 6 being the highest possible score and 1 being the lowest.

Title and author of essay: _____

Source: _____

1. Does the writer get his/her meaning across?

   SCORE: _____

2. Does the essay have an opening and a closing?

   SCORE: _____

3. Is the essay clearly focused?

   SCORE: _____

4. Does the essay have unity?

   SCORE: _____

5. Does the essay have coherence?

   SCORE: _____

6. Has the writer developed his/her ideas well?

   SCORE: _____

7. Has the writer made effective use of details?

   SCORE: _____

8. Are there any errors in usage, sentence construction, or mechanics?

   SCORE: _____

9. Do sentences vary in structure and length?

   SCORE: _____

FYI   **How Long Should a Response Be?**

There is no "correct" length for your extended responses. Each response should be as long as necessary to accomplish the given task and meet the scoring standards (see page 128). The quality and completeness of your writing matter more than the number of words you write.

Tailor each response to the particular prompt. Make sure your writing is well organized and has a clear, single focus. Develop and support your main ideas with plenty of specific, relevant details.

Sample extended responses appear in this chapter on pages 145, 147, 156–157, and 161.

TRANSITIONAL WORDS AND PHRASES

Transitional words and phrases help readers follow a writer's thoughts. They guide readers from one sentence or paragraph to the next, smoothly connecting ideas and supporting information.

Transitional words and phrases often appear at the beginning of a sentence. However, they may also come in the middle or even at the end of a sentence.

PURPOSE	WORD/PHRASE
Give an example	for example, for instance, such as, one reason, in particular

Example: *New Jersey has many tourist attractions, <u>such as</u> its scenic parks.*

Add information	also, another, furthermore, in addition, and, besides, too, as well

Example: *<u>In addition</u>, the state has numerous beautiful beaches.*

State a consequence or conclusion	because of, for this reason, therefore, consequently, as a result, finally, lastly

Example: *Lack of rain has left the woods very dry. <u>For this reason</u>, no campfires are permitted.*

Make a comparison or signal a change in direction	both, however, on the other hand, but, although, even though, otherwise, on the contrary, in contrast

Example: *Living in the country is less stressful than living in the city. <u>However</u>, city living can be exciting.*

Add emphasis	especially, in particular, in fact, above all, most important

Example: *Princeton University is an outstanding school. <u>In fact</u>, it's one of the nation's finest schools.*

Show sequence	first, second, third (and so on); next; finally; after; before; while; during; later on; then; meanwhile; at last; after a while; immediately

Example: *The storm ended in the afternoon. <u>After a while</u>, the sun came out.*

| ***Show position*** | above, across, before, behind, beside, below, farther, in front of, inside, nearby, next to, outside, over, under |

Example: *New Jersey is located <u>across</u> the Hudson River from New York.*

THE *PROCESS* OF WRITING

You've probably learned that writing is a *process* made up of several steps. When you take the Language Arts HSPA, you can use this process to plan and write your extended responses.

PLANNING
. . . prewriting: thinking and planning *before* writing

WRITING
. . . turning your plan into a draft

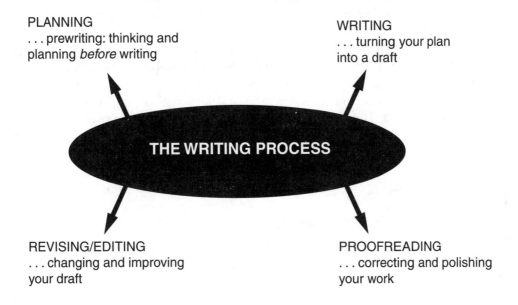

THE WRITING PROCESS

REVISING/EDITING
. . . changing and improving your draft

PROOFREADING
. . . correcting and polishing your work

There are four steps to the writing process: planning, writing, revising/editing, and proofreading. You're already familiar with these steps, because in Chapter 2 you learned how to use them to answer open-ended questions (see pages 27–29.

Let's review the steps and see how you can use them to respond to the HSPA writing prompts:

- **Step 1: *Make a plan.*** This "prewriting" step involves careful thinking and planning. You need to plan both the content and the organization of your response.

  Note that *a key part of planning is carefully reading and thinking about the writing prompt.* The prompt identifies your topic and focus, states your writing purpose, and explains exactly what you have to do.

  The box on pages 134–135 summarizes some popular planning (prewriting) techniques.

PLANNING (PREWRITING) TECHNIQUES

There are many different techniques that can help you plan and write essays and other extended responses. Try these to see which ones work for you:

- **Brainstorming** is a way to identify ideas and supporting details and examples. When you brainstorm, you list as many ideas, details, and examples as you can think of relating to your topic. Don't worry about which ones are good or bad. Just get your thoughts down on paper. Jot down words, phrases, or whole sentences in whatever order you think of them. When you have a substantial list, look it over. Mark those items you think would work best.

- **Mapping**, also called **clustering** or **diagramming**, is a technique that helps you visualize what you're going to write. Using some combination of circles, boxes, lines, and arrows, you create a picture of the ideas and supporting information you plan to include. Because mapping helps you see relationships between ideas and details, it's useful not only for gathering information but also for planning how to organize it. Here's one example of what a "map" for three paragraphs of an extended response might look like:

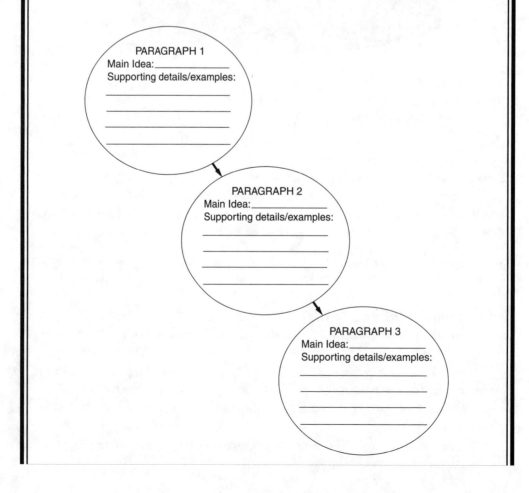

- **Outlining**, like mapping, is useful for both gathering and organizing information. When you write from an outline, you'll often find that each main idea with its supporting information becomes a separate paragraph in your draft. You can take a formal or informal approach to outlining. Compare these examples:

INFORMAL OUTLINE

IDEA
Supporting detail/example
   —related detail
   —related detail
Supporting detail/example
   —related detail
   —related detail

FORMAL OUTLINE

I. IDEA
   A. Supporting detail/example
      1. related detail
      2. related detail
   B. Supporting detail/example
      1. related detail
      2. related detail

- **Freewriting** means writing about a topic for five minutes or longer without stopping. Freewriting is similar to brainstorming in that you don't stop to judge which ideas are good or bad as you write them. You just get some thoughts down on paper. When you're finished, you can underline ideas, details, and even whole sentences to use in your extended response. Freewriting can help you get started if you can't figure out how to begin—or *re*-started if you get stuck.

FYI   **Use the Available Time Wisely**

Remember that the test administrator will tell you how much time you have to complete each part of the exam. He or she will also help you keep track of time.

Budget your planning and writing time so that you can finish each task to your satisfaction.

- **Step 2: *Write your response.*** After making a plan or outline, you're ready to start writing. You may want to change or expand your original plan as you go along. That's fine.
- **Step 3: *Revise/edit.*** Once your ideas are down on paper, you can reread and evaluate what you've written. You can rearrange ideas, add or take out supporting information, change wording, and make other improvements.
- **Step 4: *Proofread.*** This final step is your chance to polish your writing. You can fix errors in grammar and punctuation, check spelling, fine-tune language, and make any other changes that you think will make your work better.

Using the Writing Process

How you carry out the steps of the writing process is up to you. For example, you might make your plan, begin writing, and then change the plan before continuing. Or, you might write a first draft and then, depending on how much time you have, a second or even a third draft. You may decide that your draft needs major revision or only light editing.

The point is that the process is flexible. Make it work for *you*. Also, remember that you won't always use the process in the same way. Some writing tasks are simpler than others. This is true for any writing you do, in school or outside of school.

For the HSPA extended responses, you may use the writing process in one way to interpret a picture and in a different way to develop a persuasive essay. Because the process is adaptable, you can adjust or expand its steps to meet the demands of a particular task and your needs as a writer.

Here's one other important point to bear in mind. *On the HSPA, the amount of time allowed for planning and writing varies from task to task.* For example, you'll have much more time to write your persuasive essay or letter (Part 5) than you will to write about a picture (Part 1). Pace yourself according to the time available.

 ## Adapting the Writing Process

Every writer has to decide for himself/herself how much time to give to each step of the writing process. Some students find that detailed planning lets them do the actual writing relatively quickly. Other students feel more comfortable making just a brief outline, dashing off a first draft, and then doing extensive revision and rewriting. You need to discover the approach that suits you best.

However, here are two firm guidelines: (1) *Always* do at least some basic planning before you start to write, and (2) *always* allow some time to reread your work and make necessary changes and corrections.

Activity B: Thinking About the Writing Process

Answer the following questions about the writing process.

1. How can approaching writing as a *process* help you do your best as a writer?

   _____

   _____

   _____

   _____

2. In what ways is the writing process "flexible"?

_____

_____

_____

Referring to the "Writer's Checklist"

As you carry out the HSPA writing tasks, you'll have a copy of the "Writer's Checklist" to refer to. This checklist, created by the New Jersey Department of Education, will help you keep in mind the scoring standards used to evaluate your extended written responses (discussed on pages 128–131).

Take a moment now to study the checklist below.

WRITER'S CHECKLIST

Important Points to Remember as You Write
and Critically Read to Revise/Edit Your Writing

CONTENT/ORGANIZATION

_____ 1. Focus on your purpose for writing and your audience. Convince your readers (audience) that your point of view, solution, or causes and/or effects are reasonable.

_____ 2. Support your point of view, solution, or causes and/or effects with details and evidence.

_____ 3. Put your ideas in the order that best communicates what you are trying to say.

SENTENCE CONSTRUCTION

_____ 4. Use clear and varied sentences.

USAGE

_____ 5. Use words correctly.

MECHANICS

_____ 6. Capitalize, spell, and punctuate correctly.

_____ 7. Write neatly.

NEW JERSEY STATE DEPARTMENT OF EDUCATION
MARCH 1999

Notice that the checklist is meant to help you write *and* revise/edit your work. In other words, you can use the checklist *throughout* the writing process.

Activity C: Understanding the "Writer's Checklist"

Compare the "Writer's Checklist" with the "Scoring Standards for Extended Responses" on page 128.

1. How are the two similar?

   _____

   _____

2. How are the two different?

   _____

   _____

3. How can using the "Writer's Checklist" help you when you take the HSPA?

   _____

   _____

REVIEW

Here's a brief summary of what you've learned in section 4.1. To review any of these points in detail, turn to the pages shown.

Content and organization (pages 128–133):

→ Your written responses should be clearly focused on your topic. Main ideas should be well developed with specific, relevant supporting information.

→ In general, responses should have three parts. The opening introduces the topic and the central idea. The body supports and develops the central idea. The closing summarizes or reinforces the most important ideas or otherwise brings the composition to a conclusion.

→ To have unity, writing must communicate a clear central idea, and every paragraph must relate to that idea.

→ For writing to be coherent, ideas must blend together into a smoothly flowing whole.

→ Use transitional words and phrases to connect ideas and details.

The writing process (pages 133–136):

→ You can use the writing process to plan and write your responses. The process has four steps: planning, writing, revising/editing, and proofreading.

→   A key part of planning is thinking about the writing prompt. The prompt identifies your focus, states your purpose, and explains what you have to do.

Activity D: Reviewing Terms

In your own words, define each of the following terms. Write complete sentences.

1. *prompt*:

    _____

    _____

    _____

2. *unity*:

    _____

    _____

    _____

3. *coherence*:

    _____

    _____

    _____

SPECULATING

The first HSPA prompt that requires you to write an extended response is linked to a picture. Specifically, your writing task is to study the picture and speculate about its meaning. *Speculate* means "to think carefully in order to draw a tentative conclusion."

Speculating is much like inferring (see section 3.2, "Making Inferences and Drawing Conclusions," pages 60–79). You combine the information that you're given with your knowledge, experience, and judgment to form a conclusion. However, when you speculate about a picture, you also need to use your imagination. For this reason, your response is a form of *creative* writing.

Speculating About a Picture

Combine . . .	*with . . .*	*to form . . .*
information from the picture	your knowledge, experience, and imagination	conclusions about what you see

Study the picture below and the writing prompt that follows. Do not write your response yet. You'll have a chance to do that later.

Writing Task:

It's often said that a picture is worth a thousand words. Regardless of an artist's or photographer's intention, what one person sees in a picture may be very different from what others see.

How would you describe the events in this picture? Use your imagination and your experience to speculate about what is happening.

Look carefully at the picture on page 140. Pay attention to details. What do you think is happening? What story does the picture suggest?

Activity E: Speculating About a Picture

In just a sentence or two, tell what you think is going on in the picture.

_____

_____

Developing Your Response

As you reflect on the picture, you're ready to put the writing process into action. Basic guidelines for doing this are summarized below. To review these guidelines in more detail, reread pages 133–136 in section 4.1.

You'll also find it helpful to review pages 27–29 in Chapter 2. However, keep in mind that the extended responses you write for Parts 1 and 5 will be longer and more involved than your answers to open-ended questions (Parts 2 and 4). For this reason, you'll apply the writing process differently, as needed.

Remember, too, that these are *general* guidelines. Always tailor the writing process to your specific task and to your needs as a writer. This is especially important for Part 1 of the HSPA. Because the Part 1 task calls upon creativity and imagination, no two students will take exactly the same approach.

Step 1: Make a plan.

- Jot down your central idea and related main ideas.
- List supporting information—specific ideas and details to support and develop your main ideas.
- Number the supporting details, either in the approximate order you plan to present them or in order of importance.

 Using Your Imagination

A good way to begin speculating about a picture is to study the scene shown and imagine what events led up to it and what events might happen next.

Also, look carefully at the people (or animals) in the scene. What exactly are they doing? What does their body language tell you? Try to imagine what the people are thinking, and why.

Step 2: Write your response.

- Start by writing an opening that introduces the topic and the central idea.
- Develop your central idea and related main ideas with the supporting information that you listed in Step 1. Add additional specific details as necessary or appropriate.
- Write a closing that summarizes or reinforces the most important ideas or otherwise brings your response to a conclusion.

Step 3: Revise/edit.

- Reread and evaluate your work. Make any necessary changes or additions.
  Reminder: Refer to the "Writer's Checklist" (see page 137) to help you keep in mind the scoring standards for extended responses (see page 128).

Step 4: Proofread.

- Check for errors in grammar, punctuation, capitalization, and spelling.

Activity F: Planning a Response

Make a plan for a response to the prompt on page 140. You may want to review *Activity E* on page 141.

To review planning (prewriting) techniques, study the box on pages 134–135.

_____

_____

_____

_____

_____

_____

_____

_____

_____

_____

_____

_____

_____

_____

_____

_____

_____

_____

_____

_____

_____

_____

Looking at a Sample Plan

Let's see how one student planned a response to the prompt on page 141. Study the sample plan below. Later, you'll read the extended response based on the plan.

Note that the student's outline may contain more or less detail than yours would. *Your plan needs to be just detailed enough for you to know what you're going to write.* You can add additional details as needed during the writing process.

Also note that the student's organizational approach may differ from the approach you would have taken. As mentioned earlier, the Part 1 task calls upon creativity and imagination, so no two students will take exactly the same approach.

After you've looked at the sample plan, go on to *Activity G.*

STUDENT'S PLAN FOR EXTENDED RESPONSE

Opening:
① —photo shows Mike & Ike, famous trained animals
② —kidnappers stole Mike & Ike four days ago
  — demanded a million dollars
③ —scene in picture shows M & I after they escape

Body:
① —Sarah Stockton, Mike & Ike's owner, called police
  —police launched search
② — Mike & Ike gave kidnappers hard time
  —bit & scratched
  —kidnappers finally locked them up & took to campsite in woods
  —M & I escaped
③ —kidnappers caught
  —bites & scratches pointed to their guilt

④ —M & I tried to find way home
    —got to roadway shown in picture
    —motorist saw them & told police

Closing:
① —in photo, police have just come
② —police blocking road & surrounding M & I
    —Sarah Stockton on her way

Activity G: Examining a Plan

Answer the following questions about the student's plan.

1. What are the strengths of the plan?

   _____

   _____

   _____

   _____

   _____

   _____

2. On what main ideas did the student base the organization?

   _____

   _____

   _____

   _____

   _____

   _____

3. Explain how the supporting information and details develop the main ideas.

   _____

   _____

   _____

   _____

   _____

   _____

Examining a Response Based on a Plan

Now let's see how the plan helped the student write the extended response. First, review the student's outline. Then read the actual response, below.

Notice how the student combines details in the picture with his/her knowledge, experience, and imagination to speculate about the meaning. Also notice how the student developed and expanded the plan, adding many specific details during the writing process that had not been included in the outline.

STUDENT'S EXTENDED RESPONSE

I would speculate that the scene shown in this photo takes place after a dramatic series of events. The chimp and the dog—let's call them Mike and Ike—are highly intelligent, trained animals. They have appeared in many movies and TV shows, and children around the world adore them.

Mike and Ike's fame has made them very valuable animals. So valuable, in fact, that four days ago the pair was stolen from a trailer on a movie location. Tacked to the side of the trailer was a ransom note. The kidnappers, three not very bright minor criminals, demanded one million dollars for the animals' safe return.

Sarah Stockton, Mike and Ike's owner and trainer, was frantic when she learned of the theft of her beloved animals. Sarah immediately phoned the police. The police launched a statewide search for the famous animals.

Meanwhile, the kidnappers underestimated their victims. Mike and Ike put up a fierce struggle, biting and scratching all three kidnappers. Finally, the trio managed to lock the animals in a cage and take them to a campsite in the woods. However, within a few days, the clever animals had managed to escape. Through the bars of the cage, Ike had seized one of the kidnappers by the wrist. Mike had snatched his keys and unlocked the cage door. In a flash, both animals had fled.

The three kidnappers attempted to recapture them, but failed. Instead, they themselves were caught when an alert witness identified them as the people who had had a chimp and a dog in their van. The kidnappers' scratches and bite marks helped the police quickly establish their guilt.

While the police were questioning the kidnappers, Mike and Ike were wandering through the woods, trying to find their way home. Finally, the animals made their way to a main roadway—the one shown in the photo—and set off in search of familiar surroundings. Before long, a motorist spotted them and notified the police.

In the photo, the police cars have just arrived. They are blocking off the road and surrounding the animals, while they wait for Sarah Stockton to come and reclaim her precious animals.

The content and organization of the extended response closely follows the student's basic plan. The student develops the main ideas with specific supporting information and details.

Activity H: Evaluating a Response

1. You read about "Patterns of Development" on pages 70–72 . What patterns(s) of development did the student use in writing the response?

    _____

    _____

    _____

    _____

    _____

2. Give at least four examples of specific supporting information and details that appear in the response but not in the outline.

    _____

    _____

    _____

    _____

    _____

3. Give at least four examples of transitional words that the student used to connect ideas and help readers follow the organizational structure. (You may want to refer back to the box on pages 132–133).

    _____

    _____

4. The following questions are based on the "Scoring Standards for Extended Responses" (page 128). Use the questions to evaluate the student's response. For each question, rate the response on a scale of 1 to 6, with 6 being the highest possible score and 1 being the lowest.

    *   Does the student get his/her meaning across?

        SCORE: _____
    *   Does the response have an opening and a closing?

        SCORE: _____
    *   Is the response clearly focused?

        SCORE: _____
    *   Does the response have unity?

        SCORE: _____
    *   Does the response have coherence?

        SCORE: _____
    *   Has the student developed his/her ideas well?

        SCORE: _____
    *   Has the student made effective use of details?

        SCORE: _____

- Are there any errors in usage, sentence construction, or mechanics?

    SCORE: _____

- Do sentences vary in structure and length?

    SCORE: _____

Activity I: Comparing Responses

The extended response that appears below was written for the same prompt as the previous student response. Even though it is clearly written, this response would receive a lower score than the one on page 145.

Read the response carefully, and compare it to the previous one. Think about how and why this one falls short. Then answer the questions that follow.

In the picture, police cars appear to be following the chimp and the dog along the road. One police car seems to be keeping pace with the animals. A second car is following at a safe distance. A third police car has pulled over to the side of the road, and the officer is talking to a young man, who is probably the driver of the car stopped there.

I'd speculate that the chimp and the dog escaped from a nearby place, such as a circus or a movie set. The police located the animals (maybe with the help of the young man) and are keeping an eye on them. Since the officers aren't approaching or trying to capture the animals, I suspect they are waiting for the animals' owner or trainer to come.

1. Which of the two extended responses does a better job of developing ideas? Explain your answer.

    _____

    _____

    _____

2. Which of the two responses shows more imagination and creativity? Explain your answer.

    _____

    _____

    _____

3. What conclusions can you draw from your answers to questions 1 and 2 about how to achieve a high score on this part of the HSPA?

    _____

    _____

    _____

Keep It Neat!

Even the most brilliant writing won't get a high score if readers have trouble reading the words. Try your best to write neatly, even when writing quickly. Hard-to-read handwriting can bring down your score because readers may find it hard to follow your ideas.

REVIEW

Here's a brief summary of what you've learned in section 4.2. To review any of these points in detail, turn to the pages shown.

Speculating (pages 140–141):

→ The first writing prompt asks you to speculate about a picture. Speculating is like inferring. You combine information with knowledge, experience, and judgment to form a conclusion. To speculate about a picture, you also must use your imagination.

Developing your response (pages 141–142):

→ Use the writing process to respond to the prompt: (1) Make a plan; (2) write your response; (3) revise/edit; (4) proofread.

PRACTICE

The activities that follow will give you a chance to practice what you've learned.

Practice Activity 1

Plan and write a response for the prompt on the next page. Refer to the "Writer's Checklist" (page 137) to help you keep in mind the scoring standards. Remember to use the four steps of the writing process.

Writing Task:

What one person sees in a picture may be very different from what others see. How would you describe what is happening in this picture? Use your imagination and your experience to speculate about the events in the picture.

_____

_____

_____

_____

_____

_____

_____

_____

_____

_____

_____

_____

_____

_____

_____

_____

_____

_____

_____

_____

_____

_____

_____

_____

_____

_____

_____

_____

_____

Practice Activity 2

A. **Peer feedback**. Work with a partner. Exchange the responses you wrote for *Practice Activity 1*, and evaluate each other's work on the basis of the questions below. Make constructive and specific suggestions to help your partner improve his/her skills.

- Does the student get his/her meaning across?
- Does the response have an opening and a closing?
- Is the response clearly focused?
- Does the response have unity?
- Does the response have coherence?
- Has the student developed his/her ideas well?
- Has the student made effective use of details?
- Are there any errors in usage, sentence construction, or mechanics?
- Do sentences vary in structure and length?

B. Use your partner's comments to help you revise your response. Make whatever changes you think will improve your work.

WRITING A PERSUASIVE ESSAY OR LETTER

Your second extended response for the HSPA is a persuasive essay or letter. The writing prompt describes a controversial issue and asks you to present your views. The issue may involve a disagreement between people, an argument over school or community affairs, or a dispute about laws or other matters affecting society in general.

In addition to describing the topic, the prompt identifies the audience for whom you're writing. That audience may be an individual, such as a teacher or administrator, or a group, such as the student council or the school board.

Study the sample prompt below, but **do not** write anything yet.

Writing Situation

Every year, many teachers and students express concern that there is too much subject matter to cover adequately in the time available. They say that the body of knowledge has simply grown too large to be managed in a ten-month school year. Furthermore, the two-month summer break makes it necessary for teachers to spend time reteaching content that students have forgotten over the summer. Now some state legislators have proposed expanding the school year to a full twelve months. They believe that doing so would let teachers teach more effectively and enable students to gain more knowledge. However, many people strongly object to this idea, and the proposal has become a controversial issue.

Your English teacher has asked students to write an essay explaining their opinions about this issue. What is your point of view? How would the proposed change affect you and other people?

Writing Task

Write an essay either supporting or opposing the proposal to expand the school year to a full twelve months. Use facts, examples, and other evidence to support your point of view.

The prompt has three paragraphs. The first paragraph presents the topic and the issue and gives you a context for writing. The second paragraph describes your reason for writing and your audience. The third paragraph tells you exactly what your writing task is.

Note that the second and third paragraphs also identify the form your response should take. That is, they tell you whether to write a persuasive essay or letter.

Prompt for Persuasive Writing

1st paragraph ➡ topic + issue + context
2nd paragraph ➡ reason for writing + audience
3rd paragraph ➡ directions for writing task

Activity J: Examining a Prompt

Using your own words, answer the following questions about the prompt on page 151.

1. Reread the first paragraph. Summarize the topic, issue, and context.

   _____

   _____

   _____

   _____

   _____

2. Reread the second paragraph. Describe the reason for writing and the audience.

   _____

   _____

   _____

3. Reread the third paragraph. What is the specific writing task?

   _____

   _____

   _____

Developing Your Response

Once you feel you understand the writing prompt, you're ready to plan and write your response. You can follow the same four steps you used to respond to the picture-related prompt, adapting the writing process as needed to develop your persuasive essay or letter.

However, when you respond to the persuasive-writing prompt, the process involves two additional elements:

> ➢ Before you can begin to plan your response, you must first determine your point of view. In other words, you have to *take a position* on the issue.
>
> For example, the prompt on page 151 asks you to either support or oppose the proposal to expand the school year. To help you clarify your position, the prompt asks you to think about how the proposed change would affect you and other people.

Bear in mind that *to write persuasively you must take a clear and definite position.* You can't take both sides of an argument—only one!

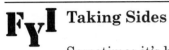 **Taking Sides**

Sometimes it's hard to figure out which side of an argument to take in a persuasive essay or letter. You may have mixed feelings about the issue.

To determine your position, list arguments for *both* sides. Then choose the side that is stronger—the side that you will be able to argue for more convincingly.

> ➢ Your main ideas and supporting information must accomplish your writing purpose. In persuasive writing, this means they must convincingly present your point of view. To be persuasive, your argument must have solid supporting reasons behind it.

To write persuasively . . .

➡ *Take a clear and definite position.*

➡ *Support your argument with solid reasons.*

Review the planning and writing steps once more, but this time think about how you would apply the process to the prompt on page 151:

THE WRITING PROCESS

Step 1: Make a plan.

- Jot down your central idea and related main ideas.
- List supporting information—specific ideas and details to support and develop your main ideas.
- Number the supporting details, either in the approximate order you plan to present them or in order of importance.

Step 2: Write your response.

- Start by writing an opening that introduces the topic and the central idea.
- Develop your central idea and related main ideas with the supporting information that you listed in Step 1. Add additional specific details as necessary or appropriate.
- Write a closing that summarizes or reinforces the most important ideas or otherwise brings your response to a conclusion.

Step 3: Revise/edit.

- Reread and evaluate your work. Make any necessary changes or additions.

Step 4: Proofread.

- Check for errors in grammar, punctuation, capitalization, and spelling.

Here's one other important point to keep in mind. When you write your persuasive essay or letter, it's helpful to clearly state each main idea in a topic sentence. (You learned about writing topic sentences to answer open-ended questions in Chapter 2.) Topic sentences help you create a sound structure for your response. They also lead readers smoothly into supporting information.

Activity K: Planning a Response

Make a plan for a response to the prompt on page 151. Remember to take a clear position and to support your point of view with solid reasons, information, and examples.

Before making your plan, you may find it helpful to review the following:

- the "Elaboration" *FYI* box on page 27
- the "Methods of Organization" feature on page 51 and the "Planning (Prewriting) Techniques" feature on pages 134–135
- the "Structure of Extended Responses" box on page 129

_____

_____

_____

_____

_____

_____

_____

_____

_____

_____

_____

_____

_____

_____

_____

_____

_____

_____

_____

_____

_____

_____

_____

Looking at a Sample Plan

Let's take a look at one student's plan for a response to the prompt on page 151. Study the sample plan below.

STUDENT'S PLAN FOR EXTENDED RESPONSE

Note: This plan may contain more or less detail than yours would. _Your plan needs to be just detailed enough for you to know what you're going to write._ You can add additional supporting information and details as needed during the writing process.

Opening: longer school year is poor idea
① —summer = valuable & well-deserved time off
② —students need time to recharge
③ —benefits of break outweigh loss of education time

Summer = time of opportunity
① —chance to relax & unwind
② —chance to:
    —try experiences
    —see places
    —meet people
③ —chance to travel, go to camp, or just hang out

Summer = opportunity for family time
① —only chance for many parents & kids to share "quality" time

Summer = chance to earn money & gain work experience
① —part-time baby-sitting
② —full-time jobs in stores & camps

Summer = special time for students
① —when finish school & get "real" job, only about 2 weeks vacation

Closing:
① —if too much subject matter, try to reduce it
② —Don't expand school year!

Note how the student has taken a definite position and plans to develop that position with specific ideas and supporting information. The student has also thought about the opening and closing. Having a strong opening and closing is especially important in persuasive writing.

Establish Focus with a Thesis Statement

To establish and maintain your focus, you may want to state your position in a thesis statement before doing anything else. You may decide to use the statement as is, either as the opening sentence or elsewhere in the first paragraph. Or, you may want to revise or rewrite the sentence. That's okay. Establishing a clear focus from the start will get you moving in the right direction.

Activity L: Comparing Plans

Compare the sample plan above with the plan you made for *Activity K* (page 154). Then answer the following questions.

1. Are the plans alike or different in the position they take? Explain.

   _____

   _____

   _____

2. In what ways are the two plans similar?

   _____

   _____

   _____

3. How do the two plans differ?

   _____

   _____

   _____

Examining a Response Based on a Plan

Review the student's plan, and then read the actual extended response below. Notice how the student supports his/her position with solid reasons and examples. Notice, too, how the student developed and expanded the plan, adding details that had not been included in the outline.

STUDENT'S EXTENDED RESPONSE

The proposal to expand the school year is a poor idea that would deprive students of valuable and well-deserved free time. Students work hard ten months a year. They need two months off to recharge their batteries. Any educational benefit lost because of those two months is more than made up for by other benefits gained through a summer break.

Summer is a time of opportunity. It's a chance to relax and unwind after the stress of studying, taking tests, and doing homework. It's also a chance to get together with friends and family, try new experiences, see different places, and meet new people.

Many kids are lucky enough to take a trip to another state or even another country. Others visit relatives, go away to summer camp, or develop their skills through a sports-related program. Some participate in community service projects, helping underprivileged children or other people in need. But even kids who just hang out with friends, go swimming at the local pool, or take afternoon strolls through the park are still getting refreshed from the break in routine.

Summer is also an opportunity for relaxed family time. In many homes, summer is the only chance parents and kids get to spend a long period of "quality" time together. Instead of dealing with day-to-day schedules and pressures, they can just have fun. They can go on picnics, play ball, ride bikes together, or work on projects around the house.

In addition to the benefits mentioned, summer also gives kids a chance to earn money. Some kids take part-time baby-sitting jobs. Others work full time in stores and summer camps. These kids earn spending money and gain worthwhile experience in the working world.

Finally, everyone should remember that summer is a special time for students. Once they finish school and go to work in the "real" world, their vacation time shrinks from two months to about two weeks a year. One advantage of being a kid is getting a couple of months off without adult responsibilities. Let's not take that advantage away.

The summer break is valuable and important for many reasons. Taking it away from students and their families would be a sad mistake. If there is too much subject matter to cover in class, let's try to reduce it. But <u>don't</u> expand the school year.

Notice how the student begins by introducing the central idea in a single sentence: *The proposal to expand the school year is a poor idea that would deprive students of valuable and well-deserved free time.* This thesis statement clearly establishes the writer's position. (For more information about thesis statements, review the *FYI* box on page 156 and "Structure of Extended Responses" on page 129.)

Here are a few other noteworthy points:

> ➢ The student uses topic sentences to clearly present main ideas. Each topic sentence relates back to the thesis statement.

> ➢ The student supports his/her argument with specific supporting information.

> ➢ The student uses transitional words and phrases (see the box on pages 132–133) to connect ideas and guide readers. For example, the student uses *in addition* in the fifth paragraph and *finally* in the sixth paragraph.

> ➢ The response has strong opening and closing paragraphs.

Activity M: Evaluating a Response

1. How closely did the student follow his/her plan to write the actual response? Be specific.

   _____

   _____

   _____

   _____

   _____

   _____

   _____

2. In your own words, summarize the student's position. Then list the main ideas the student used to support his/her argument.

   _____

   _____

   _____

   _____

   _____

   _____

   _____

3. The following questions are based on the "Scoring Standards for Extended Responses" (page 128). Use the questions to evaluate the student's response. For each question, rate the response on a scale of 1 to 6, with 6 being the highest possible score and 1 being the lowest.

   • Does the student get his/her meaning across?

   SCORE: _____

   • Does the response have an opening and a closing?

   SCORE: _____

   • Is the response clearly focused?

   SCORE: _____

   • Does the response have unity?

   SCORE: _____

   • Does the response have coherence?

   SCORE: _____

   • Has the student developed his/her ideas well?

   SCORE: _____

- Has the student made effective use of details?

  SCORE: _____

- Are there any errors in usage, sentence construction, or mechanics?

  SCORE: _____

- Do sentences vary in structure and length?

  SCORE: _____

UNITY AND COHERENCE

Unified writing
➡ **Communicates a clear central idea**
➡ **Every paragraph relates to that idea**

Coherent writing
➡ **Clearly and logically organized**
  Flows in a way that makes sense and is easy for readers to follow
➡ **Stays focused**
  Has a clear topic and sticks to it
➡ **Smoothly connected**
  Uses transitional words and phrases to connect ideas

Activity N: Questions for Thought and Discussion

Discuss the following questions as a class or in small groups. Then write your answers.

1. In the last paragraph, the student mentions an *opposing* argument about the amount of subject matter to be taught: *If there is too much subject matter to cover in class, let's try to reduce it.* Do you think that referring to an opposing argument helps or hurts a persuasive essay? Explain your reasoning.

   _____

   _____

   _____

   _____

   _____

   _____

   _____

   _____

2. Point of view varies from person to person. The extended response on pages 156–157 presents one student's viewpoint. Do you think the following individuals would or would not be likely to share the student's opinions? Give specific reasons for your answers.

a teacher:

_____

_____

_____

_____

_____

a principal:

_____

_____

_____

_____

_____

a parent:

_____

_____

_____

_____

_____

an adult who is not a parent:

_____

_____

_____

_____

_____

3. You can use the four-step writing process to respond to the picture-related prompt and to the persuasive-writing prompt. However, you'll have to tailor your planning and writing to the specific task. Explain.

_____

_____

_____

_____

_____

Considering Alternate Approaches

When you plan and write an extended response, remember that there is no one "correct" length or approach. As long as you accomplish the given task and develop and support your ideas with plenty of specific, relevant details, you'll do well.

In the extended response on pages 156–157, the student chose to present a well-thought-out series of reasons and examples to support his/her position. Maybe you would have preferred to write a more "personal" essay. For example, writing in the first person (using such pronouns such as *I*, *me*, and *my*), you might have discussed different ways in which you and your family and friends have benefited from specific summer activities over the years.

The extended response that appears below is an *alternate* version of the one on pages 156–157. Read the response carefully, and compare it to the first version. Think about how the two responses are alike and how they differ. Then go on to *Activity O.*

STUDENT'S EXTENDED RESPONSE: ALTERNATE VERSION

I think that the proposal to expand the school year is a poor idea that would deprive students of valuable and well-deserved free time. We work hard ten months a year. We need two months off to recharge our batteries. Any educational benefit we might lose because of those two months is more than made up for by other benefits we gain through a summer break.

For me, summer is a time of opportunity. It's a chance for me to relax and unwind after the stress of studying, taking tests, and doing homework. It's also a chance to get together with my friends and family, try new experiences, see different places, and meet new people.

In past summers, some of my friends have been lucky enough to take trips to other states or even other countries. I usually visit relatives or go away to summer camp. This year I may develop my skills in a soccer program. I may also participate in a community service project, such as helping underprivileged children. But even if I do nothing else than just hang out with friends, go swimming at the local pool, or take afternoon strolls through the park, I'd still be getting refreshed from the break in routine.

Summer is also an opportunity for relaxed family time. In my home, summer is the only chance my parents and I get to spend a long period of "quality" time together. Instead of dealing with day-to-day schedules and pressures, we can just have fun. We can go on picnics, play ball, ride bikes together, or work on projects around the house.

In addition to the benefits mentioned, summer also gives me a chance to earn money. Last summer, I did a lot of baby-sitting. Maybe next summer I'll work full time in a store or a summer camp. Summer jobs let me earn spending money and gain worthwhile experience in the working world.

Finally, everyone should remember that summer is a special time for students. Once we finish school and go to work in the "real" world, our vacation time shrinks from two months to about two weeks a year. One advantage of being a kid is getting a couple of months off without adult responsibilities. Let's not take that advantage away.

The summer break is valuable and important for many reasons. Taking it away from students and their families would be a sad mistake. If there is too much subject matter to cover in class, let's try to reduce it. But <u>don't</u> expand the school year.

Activity O: Comparing Responses

Compare the two versions of the extended response (pages 156–157 and 161–162). Then answer the questions below.

1. How are the two versions alike? How are they different? Be specific.

    _____

    _____

    _____

    _____

2. Which of the two extended responses do you like better? Why?

    _____

    _____

    _____

3. Review your scores for question 3 of *Activity M* on page 158. Would you give this version of the response exactly the same scores? Explain your answer.

    _____

    _____

    _____

    _____

4. What conclusions can you draw from your answers to questions 1–3?

    _____

    _____

    _____

    _____

REVIEW

Here's a brief summary of what you've learned in section 4.3. To review any of these points in detail, turn to the pages shown.

Writing a persuasive essay or letter (pages 151–152):

→ The second writing prompt describes a controversial issue and asks you to present your views in a persuasive essay or letter.

→ Besides describing the topic, the prompt gives you a context for writing and identifies your audience.

Developing your response (pages 152–154):

→ Use the writing process to respond to the prompt: (1) Make a plan; (2) write your response; (3) revise/edit; (4) proofread.

→ Before beginning to plan, you must first determine your point of view. That is, you must take a clear and definite position on the issue.

→ To write persuasively, support your argument with solid reasons and specific information and details.

→ Having a strong opening and closing is especially important in persuasive writing.

PRACTICE

The activities that follow will give you a chance to practice what you've learned.

Practice Activity 1

Plan and write a response for the prompt below. Refer to the "Writer's Checklist" (page 137) to help you keep in mind the scoring standards.

Remember to use the four steps of the writing process. Also remember the suggestion discussed in the *FYI* box on page 156: you may find it helpful to state your position in a thesis statement before doing anything else.

Writing Situation

Candy bars, chips, cookies, soda, and other junk food is available for purchase in high school vending machines and in the cafeteria. A growing number of parents are urging school administrators to remove such foods from school grounds. These parents feel that by selling junk food, schools are sending students a poor message about what makes up a healthful diet. Furthermore, the parents are concerned that students are spending their lunch money on junk rather than on nutritious foods. However, many students disagree with the parents. They feel that they are old enough to make their own decisions about what they eat.

You've decided to write a letter to the school board voicing your opinions about this issue. What is your point of view? How would the proposed ban on junk food affect you and other students?

Writing Task

Write a letter to the school board either supporting or opposing the proposed removal of junk food from school grounds. Use facts, examples, and other evidence to support your point of view.

_____
_____
_____
_____
_____
_____
_____
_____
_____
_____
_____
_____
_____
_____
_____
_____
_____
_____
_____
_____
_____
_____
_____
_____
_____
_____
_____
_____
_____
_____
_____

Practice Activity 2

A. **Peer feedback**. Work with a partner. Exchange the responses you wrote for *Practice Activity 1*, and evaluate each other's work on the basis of the questions below. Make constructive and specific suggestions to help your partner improve his/her skills.

- Does the student get his/her meaning across?
- Does the response have an opening and a closing?
- Is the response clearly focused?
- Does the response have unity?
- Does the response have coherence?
- Has the student developed his/her ideas well?
- Has the student made effective use of details?
- Are there any errors in usage, sentence construction, or mechanics?
- Do sentences vary in structure and length?

B. Use your partner's comments to help you revise your response. Make whatever changes you think will improve your work.

4.4 THE REVISE/EDIT TASK

REVISING AND EDITING

In addition to writing extended responses, you'll be asked to revise and edit the first draft of a student-written essay. The essay will contain a variety of errors in grammar and usage, sentence construction, punctuation, and the like. Your task is to improve and correct the essay while preserving the writer's ideas. In other words, *you can revise, edit, and rewrite the writer's words, but you should not change the writer's meaning.*

Your work will be scored on the basis of essentially the same standards used to evaluate your extended responses, including:

- content and organization
- usage
- sentence construction
- mechanics

To review the elements that make up these standards, see page 128.

As you carry out the revise/edit task, you'll have a copy of the "Revising/ Editing Guide" to help you. This guide shows simple ways to mark text and lists the kinds of errors and problems that you should watch for as you work on the text. Take a moment to examine the guide below.

Revising/Editing Guide

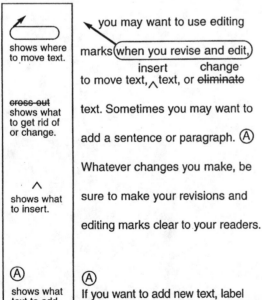

shows where to move text.

cross out shows what to get rid of or change.

∧ shows what to insert.

Ⓐ shows what text to add and where to add it.

you may want to use editing marks (when you revise and edit,) to move text, ∧ insert text, or eliminate change text. Sometimes you may want to add a sentence or paragraph. Ⓐ

Whatever changes you make, be sure to make your revisions and editing marks clear to your readers.

Ⓐ If you want to add new text, label the new text with a letter or number. Then write the label to show where you are adding it.

What to consider when you revise and edit:

CONTENT/ORGANIZATION
1. opening and closing
2. development of key ideas
3. logical progression of ideas
4. supporting details
5. transitions

SENTENCE CONSTRUCTION
6. correct sentence structure (syntax)
7. varied sentence structure

USAGE
8. correct verb tenses
9. subject/verb agreement
10. pronoun usage and agreement
11. word choice

MECHANICS
12. spelling
13. capitalization
14. punctuation

For now, just look at the following sample prompt and essay. **Do not make corrections yet**. Then go on to *Activity P,* which follows.

Task:

Some parents and educators have criticized what they see as too much emphasis on high school sports. They feel that schools should cut back on athletics and focus more on academic matters.

One student has written an essay for his local newspaper expressing his views on this controversial issue. Read his first draft and think about how to improve the text. Then make your revisions.

Comunitys over emfasize high school sports schools spend to much money on to many sports and there is to much talk about games, teams, and athleets

Instead of for coaches, equippment, and other sports expenses most of the money that schools spend should be for educational stuff. Good education. That's whats important to students not instruction in bats and balls. Only a small some of money is what should be set aside. For a few sports.

Sports is not importent enuf for to be deserving so much atenshun. many students are not intrested in athleticks And many is simply not good athletes. Yet, everyone is constantly hears about games and reads about athletes in the newspaper.

Emfasizing sports send a rong messege to kids in real life it doesnt matter at all if you can score a gole or score a basket. What is matter is knowledge. And understanding. But won-lost records, seems to get about twice as much atenshun as accademick acheivmints.

Its time for to set the prioritys strait. Lets reduce the time energy and money devoting to sports. And focus to education instead.

Activity P: Evaluating a First Draft

1. Read the prompt and the student's first-draft essay above. Think about the following points:

    *   Does the student get his/her meaning across?
    *   Does the response have an opening and a closing?
    *   Is the response clearly focused?
    *   Does the response have unity?
    *   Does the response have coherence?
    *   Has the student developed his/her ideas well?
    *   Has the student made effective use of details?
    *   Are there any errors in usage, sentence construction, or mechanics?
    *   Do sentences vary in structure and length?

2. What do you think are the greatest weaknesses of the essay?

_____

_____

_____

_____

_____

_____

3. What do you think are the essay's strengths?

_____

_____

_____

_____

_____

_____

FYI Mark up or Re-copy

Revising and editing can get messy. When you make changes, insert text, or rearrange sentences, do it as neatly and clearly as you can. _Readers must be able to understand your revisions for you to get a high score._

Here's an even better idea. Once you've finished working on the draft, re-copy the entire edited essay onto your answer sheet.

Making Revisions

To revise a draft, look for places to clarify meaning and improve writing flow. Add or delete words as needed. Develop ideas and information where necessary. Fix wording that is vague or confusing. Rearrange phrases, sentences, or even paragraphs to improve organization.

You'll probably find it helpful to concentrate first on content and organization and deal with mechanics later. But don't underestimate the importance of correct grammar, punctuation, and the like. "Small" errors interfere with the flow of writing and make it difficult for readers to read and understand a paper.

The student's first draft on page 167 has plenty of room for improvement. Let's see how you might begin to revise/edit the student's work.

Study the first two revised/edited paragraphs of the essay below. Notice how editing marks serve to show the changes. Bear in mind that if _you_ were editing the draft, your changes might differ from the ones shown.

Communities overemphasize
~~Comunitys over emfasize~~ high school sports schools spend to much money on to

many sports and there is to much talk about games, teams, and ~~athleets~~ *athletes*.

~~Instead of~~ (for coaches, equipment, and other sports expenses) most of the

money that schools spend should be for educational *used* ~~stuff. Good education~~. *materials instead*. A top-quality

education is what's
~~That's whats~~ important to students, not instruction in ~~bats and~~ balls. Only a *swinging a bat or kicking a*

small *sum* ~~some~~ of money ~~is what~~ should be set aside ~~For~~ *for* a few sports.

With so many changes, this student may want to re-copy the entire edited essay onto his/her answer sheet, if there's enough time. A clean, neat copy would be much easier for readers to read.

Activity Q: Thinking About Revisions

Carefully compare the revised/edited paragraphs above with the original paragraphs on page 167. Think about what changes were made and why. Then answer the following questions.

1. How did the changes improve the first draft? Be specific.

    _____
    _____
    _____
    _____
    _____
    _____
    _____

2. What might you have done differently?

    _____
    _____
    _____
    _____
    _____
    _____
    _____

Improve Your Skills

When you're revising, editing, and proofreading, here are some of the most common errors to guard against:

- confusing organization
- lack of transition words
- sentence fragments
- run-on sentences
- subject and verb do not agree
- pronoun and antecedent do not agree
- sentence structure is not parallel
- misspelled words
- missing or incorrect punctuation

If any of these give you trouble, make an effort to improve your skills. For example, review your papers and identify words you often spell incorrectly. Memorize the correct spellings. Or, if you have trouble with run-on sentences, subject-verb agreement, or the like, ask your teacher for help.

REVIEW

Here's a brief summary of what you've learned in section 4.4. To review any of these points in detail, turn to the pages shown.

Revising and editing (pages 166–169):

→ For the revise/edit task, you have to improve the writing while preserving the writer's ideas. You can revise and rewrite, but you should not change the meaning.

→ Look for places to clarify meaning and improve writing flow. Add, delete, change, or rearrange words as needed.

→ You'll probably find it helpful to focus on content and organization first, mechanics second. Remember, though, that "small" errors interfere with readers' ability to understand a paper.

→ Use editing marks to clearly show the changes you are making.

PRACTICE

The activities that follow will give you a chance to practice what you've learned.

Practice Activity 1

The prompt and first-draft essay that you first saw on page 167 appear again below. Carry out the revise/edit task as described. Refer to the "Revising/ Editing Guide" on page 166 to help you.

You can look back at the sample editing shown on page 169. However, you should make the changes and improvements that *you* think are necessary and appropriate.

Task:

Some parents and educators have criticized what they see as too much emphasis on high school sports. They feel that schools should cut back on athletics and focus more on academic matters.

One student has written an essay for his local newspaper expressing his views on this controversial issue. Read his first draft and think about how to improve the text. Then make your revisions.

Comunitys over emfasize high school sports schools spend to much money on to many sports and there is to much talk about games, teams, and athleets

Instead of for coaches, equippment, and other sports expenses most of the money that schools spend should be for educational stuff. Good education. That's whats important to students not instruction in bats and balls. Only a small some of money is what should be set aside. For a few sports.

Sports is not importent enuf for to be deserving so much atenshun. many students are not intrested in athleticks And many is simply not good athletes. Yet, everyone is constantly hears about games and reads about athletes in the newspaper.

Emfasizing sports send a rong messege to kids in real life it doesnt matter at all if you can score a gole or score a basket. What is matter is knowledge. And understanding. But won-lost records, seems to get about twice as much atenshun as accademick acheivmints.

Its time for to set the prioritys strait. Lets reduce the time energy and money

devoting to sports. And focus to education instead.

Practice Activity 2

A. **Work with a partner.** Compare the changes that you made to the student's essay. Discuss similarities and differences.

B. **Peer feedback.** Evaluate each other's work on the basis of content and organization, usage, sentence construction, and mechanics. Make constructive and specific suggestions to help your partner improve his/her skills.

HSPA IN LANGUAGE ARTS LITERACY: PRACTICE TESTS 1 AND 2

REMINDER:

- As you carry out the extended writing tasks, you may refer to the **Writer's Checklist** and the **Revising/Editing Guide** (page 174).

WRITER'S CHECKLIST

Important Points to Remember as You Write
and Critically Read to Revise/Edit Your Writing

CONTENT/ORGANIZATION

_____ 1. Focus on your purpose for writing and your audience. Convince your readers (audience) that your point of view, solution, or causes and/or effects are reasonable.

_____ 2. Support your point of view, solution, or causes and/or effects with details and evidence.

_____ 3. Put your ideas in the order that best communicates what you are trying to say.

SENTENCE CONSTRUCTION

_____ 4. Use clear and varied sentences.

USAGE

_____ 5. Use words correctly.

MECHANICS

_____ 6. Capitalize, spell, and punctuate correctly.

_____ 7. Write neatly.

NEW JERSEY STATE DEPARTMENT OF EDUCATION
MARCH 1999

Revising/Editing Guide

shows where to move text.

~~cross out~~ shows what to get rid of or change.

∧ shows what to insert.

Ⓐ shows what text to add and where to add it.

you may want to use editing marks (when you revise and edit,) to move text, ∧ insert text, or ~~eliminate~~ change text. Sometimes you may want to add a sentence or paragraph. Ⓐ

Whatever changes you make, be sure to make your revisions and editing marks clear to your readers.

Ⓐ If you want to add new text, label the new text with a letter or number. Then write the label to show where you are adding it.

What to consider when you revise and edit:

CONTENT/ORGANIZATION
1. opening and closing
2. development of key ideas
3. logical progression of ideas
4. supporting details
5. transitions

SENTENCE CONSTRUCTION
6. correct sentence structure (syntax)
7. varied sentence structure

USAGE
8. correct verb tenses
9. subject/verb agreement
10. pronoun usage and agreement
11. word choice

MECHANICS
12. spelling
13. capitalization
14. punctuation

LANGUAGE ARTS LITERACY: PART 1

Writing Task:

What one person sees in a picture may be very different from what others see. How would you describe what is happening in this picture? Use your imagination and your experience to speculate about the events in the picture.

_____

_____

_____

_____

_____

_____

_____

_____

_____

LANGUAGE ARTS LITERACY: PART 2

DIRECTIONS: Read the selection and answer the questions that follow.

Once they leave school, many people stop reading books. In this essay, the writer presents her views on this situation.

Why Reading Counts
by Cynthia M. Leary

A recent survey listed some astounding figures: 20 percent of American adults are illiterate, and 50 percent of adults who *can* read say that they "never read books." We are all willing to agree that illiteracy is a serious problem, one that schools must work hard to solve. After all, citizens need reading skills to get decent jobs, to fill out tax forms, to read road signs—to survive in the modern world. But does it matter that half of all Americans don't read books? Surely there are more important things to worry about.

But we should worry. People today need answers, perhaps more desperately than ever. In a world beset by the catastrophes of overpopulation and pollution, a world in which people feel the press of the nuclear knife at their throats, we need answers. We also need answers to the questions that have always troubled humanity, those questions which may sound like clichés but which are nevertheless haunting and real: Why does evil exist? What is the purpose of my life? Do I have obligations to other people?

No single, magical book, of course, provides all the answers we need. But reading can be the key that unlocks solutions. First of all, reading can make us *aware*. *Uncle Tom's Cabin* may seem tainted with sentimentality today, but to its original readers it brought the horror of slavery to vivid and unforgettable life. Rachel Carson's exposé of the grim effects of pesticides, *Silent Spring*, came as a revelation to readers when it was published in 1962: few people had known that the powders we sprayed on plants and pests were making their way back to us in a circular pathway of poison. Betty Friedan's book *The Feminine Mystique* told the world about a secret women had hidden for a long time: the daily companions of many dutiful housewives were boredom, frustration, and resentment. These three books, and many others, had a real influence on their times. They helped trigger mass movements in society, from abolitionism to environmentalism to women's liberation. However, the power of books to expose and to explain exists only if people read them.

Reading also helps us *know ourselves*. Novelists, short-story writers, and poets compel us to explore our own interior selves as we read. Anyone who has ever said, while reading, "That's exactly how I feel" or "I know this character" or "How could this author know so much about my own life?" has experienced what Thomas DeQuincy called the "literature of power." We discover that communication can exist across cultural boundaries—indeed, across the boundaries of time itself. The universal experiences and emotions of being human bind author and reader in a shared journey toward understanding. Reading is an important way to explore what it is to be human and to find possible answers for the ethical and moral questions we ask ourselves.

If reading is so valuable, why do people avoid it? Why do half of us consider it drudgery rather than pleasure? In today's world, there are many excuses for not reading:

I don't have time. Most people trap themselves in a daily scramble to keep up with responsibilities. They rush from work to home, from meeting to shopping center, from errand to errand. They simply don't have time, they think, to spend hours with a book. There are more important things to do.

I'm a slow reader. For many, reading is an almost painful experience. Such people may have been taught to read by teachers who emphasized mistakes rather than accomplishments. They remember the terror of reading aloud, of stumbling over words, of being corrected and feeling humiliated. Reading became a frustrating activity; every book was a minefield of unknown words and tangled sentences. As adults, these people find reading to be a slow, difficult, plodding business.

There's something good on television right now. After a hard day, Americans unwind with television. It's non-threatening, understandable, and pleasant. In contrast, sitting down with a book means concentrating. It means grappling with ideas, trying to understand plot and characters—with never a commercial break. The passivity of television is more appealing than the strenuous mental activity of reading.

Reading is too hard. Some people are willing to bypass the excuse television supplies and simply state baldly that they don't want to do the hard work reading requires. And they are right. Reading *is* hard. Deciphering printed words and letters, making sense of grammatical structure, and following another person's thought patterns are <u>daunting</u> tasks. Even psychologists and linguists admit that reading is one of the human brain's most mysterious skills; they are at a loss to explain exactly how people learn to read. Many people would rather avoid such a demanding activity.

9

Reading is a waste of time. Some people feel that reading "for pleasure" (anything not directly connected to a job or immediately practical) is a waste of valuable time. Spending hours with a book, they think, is unproductive dreaming. For example, when politicians and business executives are asked about their reading, they often reply proudly, "I keep up with the professional literature, but I don't have time for books." Their tone implies that anyone with time to read books is, somehow, a shirker or an idler.

The idea that reading is a waste of time may also stem from a person's family background. If the adults in a family never spend time reading, the children may absorb the idea that reading is not a respected or valued activity.

There are important arguments that must be made against this rather formidable list of excuses for not reading:

There is time to read. Obviously, people make time for the things they consider important. Now that we've gone fitness-mad, for instance, millions of us have made time in our busy lives to jog or to attend exercise classes. If a person is convinced that reading is vital, then he or she will find the time to read.

Slow readers can speed up. A person who once endured the agonies of a reading class—reading each and every word, fearing mistakes, being afraid to guess—should forget all these "rules." There is no need, for example, to read every word slowly and carefully or to turn to the dictionary each time an unfamiliar word crops up. Slow readers should follow the example of good readers, who read for meaning. Good readers take in clusters of words at a time and depend on context to clarify unfamiliar words. Slow readers should find material that intrigues and involves them; then, the words will begin to flow more quickly and easily. In one respect, reading is like many physical skills: people improve when they combine frequent practice with relaxed concentration.

No one has to give up television. Television serves a fine purpose as a mild tranquilizer. We all need a break now and then from the important matters of our lives and television can provide an easy and harmless release. The problem, though, is that television is beginning to dominate our lives and those of our children. In 1980, for example, almost 70 percent of 233,000 sixth-graders polled by the California Department of Education reported that they rarely read for pleasure; the same percentage stated that they watched television four or more hours a day. Television, despite its occasional foray into quality programming, cannot replace reading. Television is overview, while reading is detail. Television reduces all to a single numbing level, while reading involves our emotions in individual human stories.

Reading is worth the work it requires. Reading is indeed hard work. But many things that we might want to do—getting into shape, learning to play a musical instrument, becoming a proficient tennis player—are difficult. We do them not because they are easy but because we want the joy and satisfaction they bring. Once we experience the pleasure and power of books, the mental stretch involved in reading becomes more than worth the effort.

16

Reading may be the best possible use of time. The issues that confront us now—genetic engineering, abortion, nuclear arms, capital punishment, euthanasia—are complex. If we, and the political leaders we elect, are to make sound decisions, we must read. We have to know about the scientific developments and ethical issues that will have an impact on our lives. Moreover, we must read in order to stir our imaginations and our emotions—particularly our empathy. Reading is the only way we can know what it might be like to be a survivor of a nuclear holocaust, a scientist with the power to shape life itself, an unwed mother, a murderer. By forcing us, in a sense, to enter minds unlike our own and worlds beyond our reach, reading frees us from the narrow confines of our own experience. We must have this kind of understanding if we are to live in a society that makes sense, a place with the potential for peace.

We have all heard the story of how the young, impoverished Abraham Lincoln trekked miles to borrow books from a neighbor and then read them by firelight. We know that nineteenth-century readers would rush to the wharf to greet the ship carrying the latest chapters of a Dickens novel. Today, reading seems less urgent and less exciting to many of us. Worse, few people impart a passion for books to their children. Instead, they leave the children in front of the television and hope, weakly, that too much watching won't be bad for them. But we cannot afford to stop reading. Books shed a light that illuminates our problems and crises. They are also mirrors that reflect the truest image of ourselves.

1. The word **tainted** in paragraph 3 means

    A. improved.
    B. spoiled.
    C. confused.
    D. strengthened.

2. To present her viewpoint convincingly, the author

    A. uses a rhetorical question to introduce each key point.
    B. appeals to emotion, rather than reason.
    C. organizes facts and details chronologically.
    D. states reasons for not reading, then argues against them.

3. As used in paragraph 9, the word **daunting** means

    A. challenging or intimidating.
    B. exciting and enjoyable.
    C. simple and easy.
    D. unnecessary or unsuitable.

4. Which statement BEST expresses the central idea of the essay?

    A. People have many sound reasons for not reading.
    B. People should read books if they can find the time.
    C. There are more arguments against reading than for it, and many are quite sound.
    D. People should read books because reading is important and worthwhile.

5. When the author describes the world as a place where "people feel the press of the nuclear knife at their throats" (paragraph 2), she is using

    A. understatement.
    B. metaphor.
    C. alliteration.
    D. satire.

6. Which of the following would the author be most likely to support?

    A. less emphasis in schools on reading books
    B. children having television sets in their bedrooms
    C. more government funding for libraries
    D. simpler books that require less thought

7. The word **beset** in paragraph 2 means

    A. encouraged.
    B. exhausted.

    C. modernized.
    D. troubled.

8. The author believes that

    A. many parents fail to encourage their children to read.
    B. watching television serves no purpose.
    C. today's books are less inspiring that those of the past.
    D. the main value of reading is as a job skill.

9. In paragraph 3, the author refers to *Uncle Tom's Cabin*, *Silent Spring*, and *The Feminine Mystique*. Which of the following positions does the author use these examples to support?

    A. Reading increases people's awareness of issues and concerns.
    B. Reading books is hard work.
    C. Reading seems less exciting to today's readers than to nineteenth-century readers.
    D. Illiteracy is a serious problem.

10. When the author refers to the "passivity of television" (paragraph 8), she means that watching television

    A. is a fine way to relax.
    B. offers those who cannot read a way to learn.
    C. requires little if any active thinking.
    D. is preferable to reading.

OPEN-ENDED ITEMS

11. In paragraph 2, the author stresses the idea that people "need answers."

    *   Explain what she means by this.
    *   How can reading books help people find answers?

    Use information from the essay to support your response.

    _____

    _____

    _____

    _____

    _____

    _____

_____

_____

_____

_____

_____

_____

_____

_____

_____

_____

_____

_____

12. In paragraph 16, the author writes: "Reading is indeed hard work. But many things that we might want to do—getting into shape, learning to play a musical instrument, becoming a proficient tennis player—are difficult."

   • How is reading like the other activities that the author mentions?
   • How are the benefits of reading different from the benefits of these other activities?

Use information from the essay to support your response.

_____

_____

_____

_____

_____

_____

_____

_____

_____

_____

_____

_____

_____

_____

_____

_____

_____

_____

_____

_____

LANGUAGE ARTS LITERACY: PART 3

Writing: Revise/Edit

Some educators have spoken out against the idea of teenagers taking after-school jobs just to make extra spending money. They believe that teens should devote their time and energy to schoolwork and extracurricular activities.

One student has written an essay for her local newspaper expressing her views on this issue. Read her first draft and think about how to improve the text. Then make your revisions.

Teenagers could have part-time jobs but not more than about five or ten hours a week working longer than that has many negitive effects.

it is understandable to need extra spending money. Working after school is a way in order to do that. However too much work is using up time and energy. That teens should be devoting to school. In a result, they either don't finish their studying and homework asignments. Or are not doing them good. Even more, demanding jobs leaves the kids real tired making them not to do their best in class

Also, its just imposible to do sports and other extracurricular stuff with long hours of work. The teen worker also miss out on time they might otherwise be spending with friends or just spend by themselves: relaxing. Furthermore, it is very stressing to be trying to do schoolwork, handle a job, and meet all the other demands of daily life.

There's one other factor to consider as well teens who are always think about earning cash often develops warped values, they become more conserned with buying clothes, CDs, and other stuff than with anything

Part-time jobs for teenagers is all right. As long as the hours is limited, strictly. If not the teen workers may gain a pocketful of change, but they loose out on a bunch of things. Things that is more importanter.

LANGUAGE ARTS LITERACY: PART 4

Directions: Read the selection and answer the questions that follow.

The responsibilities that we are given or that we take upon ourselves can have a big impact on our lives. The following story explores this idea through the experience of a young teenage girl and her brother.

Raymond's Run
by Toni Cade Bambara

I don't have much work to do around the house like some girls. My mother does that. And I don't have to earn my pocket money by hustling; George runs errands for the big boys and sells Christmas cards. And anything else that's got to get done, my father does. All I have to do in life is mind my brother Raymond, which is enough.

Sometimes I slip and say my little brother Raymond. But as any fool can see he's much bigger and he's older too. But a lot of people call him my little brother cause he needs looking after cause he's not quite right. And a lot of smart mouths got lots to say about that too, especially when George was minding him. But now, if anybody has anything to say to Raymond, anything to say about his big head, they have to come by me. And I don't play the dozens or believe in standing around with somebody in my face doing a lot of talking. I much rather just knock you down and take my chances even if I am a little girl with skinny arms and a squeaky voice, which is how I got the name Squeaky. And if things get too rough, I run. And as anybody can tell you, I'm the fastest thing on two feet.

There is no track meet that I don't win the first place medal. I used to win the twenty-yard dash when I was a little kid in kindergarten. Nowadays, it's the fifty-yard dash. And tomorrow I'm subject to run the quarter-meter relay all by myself and come in first, second, and third. The big kids call me Mercury cause I'm the swiftest thing in the neighborhood. Everybody knows that—except two people who know better, my father and me. He can beat me to Amsterdam Avenue with me having a two fire-hydrant headstart and him running with his hands in his pockets and whistling. But that's private information. Cause can you imagine some thirty-five-year-old man stuffing himself into PAL shorts to race little kids? So as far as everyone's concerned, I'm the fastest and that goes for Gretchen, too, who has put out the tale that she is going to win the first-place medal this year. Ridiculous.

In the second place, she's got short legs. In the third place, she's got freckles. In the first place, no one can beat me and that's all there is to it.

I'm standing on the corner admiring the weather and about to take a stroll down Broadway so I can practice my breathing exercises, and I've got Raymond walking on the inside close to the buildings, cause he's subject to fits of fantasy and starts thinking he's a circus performer and that the curb is a tightrope strung high in the air. And sometimes after a rain he likes to step down off his tightrope right into the gutter and slosh around getting his shoes and cuffs wet. Then I get hit when I get home. Or sometimes if you don't watch him he'll dash across traffic to the island in the middle of Broadway and give the pigeons a fit. Then I have to go behind him apologizing to all the old people sitting around trying to get some sun and getting all upset with the pigeons fluttering around them, scattering their newspapers and upsetting the waxpaper lunches in their laps. So I keep Raymond on the inside of me, and he plays like he's driving a stagecoach which is O.K. by me so long as he doesn't run me over or interrupt my breathing exercises, which I have to do on account of I'm serious about my running, and I don't care who knows it.

Now some people like to act like things come easy to them, won't let on that they practice. Not me. I'll high-prance down 34th Street like a rodeo pony to keep my knees strong even if it does get my mother uptight so that she walks ahead like she's not with me, don't know me, is all by herself on a shopping trip, and I am somebody else's crazy child. Now you take Cynthia Procter for instance. She's just the opposite. If there's a test tomorrow, she'll say something like, "Oh, I guess I'll play handball this afternoon and watch television tonight," just to let you know she ain't thinking about the test. Or like last week when she won the spelling bee for the millionth time, "A good thing you got 'receive,' Squeaky, cause I would have got it wrong. I completely forgot about the spelling bee." And she'll clutch the lace on her blouse like it was a narrow escape. Oh, brother. But of course when I pass her house on my early morning trots around the block, she is practicing the scales on the piano over and over and over and over. Then in music class she always lets herself get bumped around so she falls accidently on purpose onto the piano stool and is so surprised to find herself sitting there that she decides just for fun to try out the ole keys. And what do you know—Chopin's waltzes just spring out of her fingertips and she's the most surprised thing in the world. A regular <u>prodigy</u>. I could kill people like that. I stay up all night studying the words for the spelling bee. And you can see me any time of day practicing running. I never walk if I can trot, and shame on Raymond if he can't keep up. But of course he does, cause if he hangs back someone's liable to walk up to him and get smart, or take his allowance from him, or ask him where he got that great big pumpkin head. People are so stupid sometimes.

So I'm strolling down Broadway breathing out and breathing in on counts of seven, which is my lucky number, and here comes Gretchen and her sidekicks: Mary Louise, who used to be a friend of mine when she first moved to Harlem from Baltimore and got beat up by everybody till I took up for her on account of her mother and my mother used to sing in the same choir when they were young girls, but people ain't grateful, so now she hangs out with the new girl Gretchen and talks about me like a dog; and Rosie, who is as fat as I am skinny and has a big mouth where Raymond is concerned and is too stupid to know that there is not a big deal of difference between herself and Raymond and that she can't afford to throw stones. So they are steady coming up Broadway and I see right away that it's going to be one of those Dodge City scenes cause the street ain't that big and they're close to the buildings just as we are. First I think I'll step into the candy store and look over the new comics and let them pass. But that's chicken and I've got a reputation to consider. So then I think I'll just walk straight on through them or even over them if necessary. But as they get to me, they slow down. I'm ready to fight, cause like I said I don't feature a whole lot of chit-chat, I much prefer to just knock you down right from the jump and save everybody a lotta precious time.

"You signing up for the May Day races?" smiles Mary Louise, only it's not a smile at all. A dumb question like that doesn't deserve an answer. Besides, there's just me and Gretchen standing there really, so no use wasting my breath talking to shadows.

"I don't think you're going to win this time," says Rosie, trying to signify with her hands on her hips all salty, completely forgetting that I have whupped her behind many times for less salt than that.

"I always win cause I'm the best," I say straight at Gretchen who is, as far as I'm concerned, the only one talking in this ventriloquist–dummy routine. Gretchen smiles, but it's not a smile, and I'm thinking that girls never really smile at each other because they don't know how and don't want to know how and there's probably no one to teach us how, cause grown-up girls don't know either. Then they all look at Raymond who has just brought his mule team to a standstill. And they're about to see what trouble they can get into through him.

"What grade you in now, Raymond?"

"You got anything to say to my brother, you say it to me, Mary Louise Williams of Raggedy Town, Baltimore."

"What are you, his mother?" <u>sasses</u> Rosie.   **12**

"That's right, Fatso. And the next word out of anybody and I'll be *their* mother too." So they just stand there and Gretchen shifts from one leg to the other and so do they. Then Gretchen puts her hands on her hips and is about to say something with her freckle-face self but doesn't. Then she walks around me looking me up and down but keeps walking up Broadway, and her sidekicks follow her. So me and Raymond smile at each other and he says, "Gidyap" to his team and I continue with my breathing exercises, strolling down Broadway toward the ice man on 145th with not a care in the world cause I am Miss Quicksilver herself.

I take my time getting to the park on May Day because the track meet is the last thing on the program. The biggest thing on the program is the May Pole dancing, which I can do without, thank you, even if my mother thinks it's a shame I don't take part and act like a girl for a change. You'd think my mother'd be grateful not to have to make me a white organdy dress with a big satin sash and buy me new white baby-doll shoes that can't be taken out of the box till the big day. You'd think she'd be glad her daughter ain't out there prancing around a May Pole getting the new clothes all dirty and sweaty and trying to act like a fairy or a flower or whatever you're supposed to be when you should be trying to be yourself, whatever that is, which is, as far as I am concerned, a poor Black girl who really can't afford to buy shoes and a new dress you only wear once a lifetime cause it won't fit next year.

I was once a strawberry in a Hansel and Gretel pageant when I was in nursery school and didn't have no better sense than to dance on tiptoe with my arms in a circle over my head doing umbrella steps and being a perfect fool just so my mother and father could come dressed up and clap. You'd think they'd know better than to encourage that kind of nonsense. I am not a strawberry. I do not dance on my toes. I run. That is what I am all about. So I

5

always come late to the May Day program, just in time to get my number pinned on and lay in the grass till they announce the fifty-yard dash.

I put Raymond in the little swings, which is a tight squeeze this year and will be impossible next year. Then I look around for Mr. Pearson, who pins the numbers on. I'm really looking for Gretchen if you want to know the truth, but she's not around. The park is jam-packed. Parents in hats and corsages and breast-pocket handkerchiefs peeking up. Kids in white dresses and light-blue suits. The parkees unfolding chairs and chasing the rowdy kids from Lenox as if they had no right to be there. The big guys with their caps on backwards, leaning against the fence swirling the basketballs on the tips of their fingers, waiting for all these crazy people to clear out the park so they can play. Most of the kids in my class are carrying bass drums and glockenspiels and flutes. You'd think they'd put in a few bongos or something for real like that.

Then here comes Mr. Pearson with his clipboard and his cards and pencils and whistles and safety pins and fifty million other things he's always dropping all over the place with his clumsy self. He sticks out in a crowd because he's on stilts. We used to call him Jack and the Beanstalk to get him mad. But I'm the only one that can outrun him and get away, and I'm too grown for that silliness now.

"Well, Squeaky," he says, checking my name off the list and handing me number seven and two pins. And I'm thinking he's got no right to call me Squeaky, if I can't call him Beanstalk.

"Hazel Elizabeth Deborah Parker," I correct him and tell him to write it down on his board.

"Well, Hazel Elizabeth Deborah Parker, going to give someone else a break this year?" I squint at him real hard to see if he is seriously thinking I should lose the race on purpose just to give someone else a break. "Only six girls running this time," he continues, shaking his head sadly like it's my fault all of New York didn't turn out in sneakers. "That new girl should give you a run for your money." He looks around the park for Gretchen like a periscope in a submarine movie. "Wouldn't it be a nice gesture if you were . . . to ahhh . . ."

I give him such a look he couldn't finish putting that idea into words. Grownups got a lot of nerve sometimes. I pin number seven to myself and stomp away, I'm so burnt. And I go straight for the track and stretch out on the grass while the band winds up with "Oh, the Monkey Wrapped His Tail Around the Flag Pole," which my teacher calls by some other name. The man on the loudspeaker is calling everyone over to the track and I'm on my back looking at the sky, trying to pretend I'm in the country, but I can't, because even grass in the city feels hard as sidewalk, and there's just no pretending you are anywhere but in a "concrete jungle" as my grandfather says.

The twenty-yard dash takes all of two minutes cause most of the little kids don't know no better than to run off the track or run the wrong way or run smack into the fence and fall down and cry. One little kid, though, has got the good sense to run straight for the white ribbon up ahead so he wins. Then the second-graders line up for the thirty-yard dash and I don't even bother to turn my head to watch cause Raphael Perez always wins. He wins before he even begins by psyching the runners, telling them they're going to trip on their shoelaces and fall on their faces or lose their shorts or something, which he doesn't really have to do since he is very fast, almost as fast as I am. After that is the forty-yard dash which I use to run when I was in the first grade. Raymond is hollering from the swings cause he knows I'm about to do my thing cause the man on the loudspeaker has just announced the fifty-yard dash, although he might just as well be giving a recipe for angel food cake cause you can hardly make out what he's sayin for the static. I get up and slip off my sweat pants and then I see Gretchen standing at the starting line, kicking her legs out like a pro. Then as I get into place I see that ole Raymond is on line on the other side of the fence, bending down with his fingers on the ground just like he knew what he was doing. I was going to yell at him but then I didn't. It burns up your energy to holler.

Every time, just before I take off in a race, I always feel like I'm in a dream, the kind of dream you have when you're sick with fever and feel all hot and weightless. I dream I'm flying over a sandy beach in the early morning sun, kissing the leaves of the trees as I fly by. And there's always the smell of apples, just like in the country when I was little and used to think I was a choo-choo train, running through the fields of corn and chugging up the hill to the orchard. And all the time I'm dreaming this, I get lighter and lighter until I'm flying over the beach again, getting blown through the sky like a feather that weighs nothing at all. But once I spread my fingers in the dirt and crouch over the Get on Your Mark, the dream goes and I am solid again and am telling myself, Squeaky you must win, you must win, you are the fastest thing in the world, you can even beat your father up Amsterdam if you really try. And then I feel my weight coming back just behind my knees then down to my feet then into the earth and the pistol shot explodes in my blood and I am off and weightless again, flying past the other runners, my arms pumping up and down and the whole world is quiet except for the crunch as I zoom over the gravel in the track. I glance to my left and there is no one. To the right, a blurred Gretchen, who's got her chin jutting out as if it would win the race all by itself. And on the other side of the fence is Raymond with his arms down to his side and the palms tucked up behind him, running in his very own style, and it's the first time I ever saw that and I almost stop to watch my brother Raymond on his first run. But the white ribbon is bouncing toward me and I tear past it, racing into the distance till my feet with a mind of their own start digging up footfuls of dirt and brake me short. Then all the kids standing on the side pile on me, banging me on the back and slapping my head with their May Day programs, for I have won again and everybody on 151st Street can walk tall for another year.

"In first place . . ." the man on the loudspeaker is clear as a bell now. But then he pauses and the loudspeaker starts to whine. Then static. And I lean down to catch my breath and here comes Gretchen walking back, for she's overshot the finish line too, huffing and puffing with her hands on her hips taking it slow, breathing in steady time like a real pro and I sort of like her a little for the first time. "In first place . . ." and then three or four voices get all mixed up on the loudspeaker and I dig my sneaker into the grass and stare at Gretchen who's staring back, we both wondering just who did win. I can hear old Beanstalk arguing with the man on the loudspeaker and then a few others running their mouths about what the stopwatches say. Then I hear Raymond yanking at the fence to call me and I wave to shush him, but he keeps rattling the fence like a gorilla in a cage like in them gorilla movies, but then like a dancer or something he starts climbing up nice and easy but very fast. And it occurs to me, watching how smoothly he climbs hand over hand and remembering how he looked running with his arms down to his side and with the wind pulling his mouth back and his teeth showing and all, it occurred to me that Raymond would make a very fine runner. Doesn't he always keep up with me on my trots? And he surely knows how to breathe in counts of seven cause he's always doing

it at the dinner table, which drives my brother George up the wall. And I'm smiling to beat the band cause if I've lost this race, or if me and Gretchen tied, or even if I've won, I can always retire as a runner and begin a whole new career as a coach with Raymond as my champion. After all, with a little more study I can beat Cynthia and her phony self at the spelling bee. And if I bugged my mother, I could get piano lessons and become a star. And I have a big rep as the baddest thing around. And I've got a roomful of ribbons and medals and awards. But what has Raymond got to call his own?

So I stand there with my new plans, laughing out loud by this time as Raymond jumps down from the fence and runs over with his teeth showing and his arms down to the side, which no one before him has quite mastered as a running style. And by the time he comes over I'm jumping up and down so glad to see him—my brother Raymond, a great runner in the family tradition. But of course everyone thinks I'm jumping up and down because the men on the loudspeaker have finally gotten themselves together and compared notes and are announcing "In first place—Miss Hazel Elizabeth Deborah Parker." (Dig that.) "In second place—Miss Gretchen P. Lewis." And I look over at Gretchen wondering what the "P" stands for. And I smile. Cause she's good, no doubt about it. Maybe she'd like to help me coach Raymond; she obviously is serious about running, as any fool can see. And she nods to congratulate me and then she smiles. And I smile. We stand there with this big smile of respect between us. It's about as real a smile as girls can do for each other, considering we don't practice real smiling every day, you know, cause maybe we too busy being flowers or fairies or strawberries instead of something honest and worthy of respect . . . you know . . . like being people.

1. Squeaky's attitude toward Raymond can best be described as

   A. indifferent.
   B. resentful.
   C. protective.
   D. mocking.

2. In paragraph 5, the narrator tells how ". . . Chopin's waltzes just spring out of her fingertips and she's the most surprised thing in the world. A regular **prodigy**." In this context, **prodigy** means

   A. someone who is conceited.
   B. a person worthy of admiration.
   C. an unusually talented musician.
   D. a deceitful person.

3. Squeaky's thoughts and actions suggest that she is

   A. angry.
   B. fearful.
   C. playful.
   D. dishonest.

4. In paragraph 12, the author writes: "'What are you, his mother?' **sasses** Rosie." In this context, **sasses** means to speak

   A. doubtfully.
   B. insolently.
   C. loudly.
   D. kindly.

5. Which of the following is an example of a simile, a literary device used in the story?

    A. "... there's just no pretending you are anywhere but in a 'concrete jungle' as my grandfather says."
    B. "The big kids call me Mercury cause I'm the swiftest thing in the neighborhood."
    C. "... I am a little girl with skinny arms and a squeaky voice, which is how I got the name Squeaky."
    D. "I'll high-prance down 34th Street like a rodeo pony to keep my knees strong. . . "

6. The main reason why Squeaky doesn't seem to have any friends is probably that she

    A. is too busy running track.
    B. spends all of her free time studying.
    C. has a shy nature.
    D. needs to look after Raymond all the time.

7. The most likely reason why the author chose the title "Raymond's Run" is to call attention to

    A. Raymond's fear of other people.
    B. Raymond's victory in the race.
    C. Squeaky's realization that her brother can run.
    D. Squeaky's decision to let Raymond run against Gretchen.

8. To make the story come alive, the author writes it in

    A. first person, present tense.
    B. first person, past tense.
    C. third person, present tense.
    D. third person, past tense.

9. Which of the following quotations best expresses the major theme of the story?

    A. "Now some people like to act like things come easy to them, won't let on that they practice."
    B. "Grownups got a lot of nerve sometimes."
    C. "All I have to do in life is mind my brother Raymond, which is enough."
    D. "And if things get too rough, I run."

10. The ending of the story implies that

    A. Squeaky will give up running.
    B. Squeaky and Gretchen may become friends.
    C. Gretchen will defeat Squeaky in the next race.
    D. Raymond can outrun Squeaky.

OPEN-ENDED ITEMS

11. A person's family situation has a significant effect on his or her life.

    • Explain how Squeaky's family situation has affected her personality.
    • How might Squeaky's life have been different if she had no brother Raymond?

    Use information from the story to support your response.

    _____

    _____

    _____

    _____

    _____

    _____

    _____

    _____

    _____

    _____

    _____

    _____

    _____

    _____

    _____

    _____

    _____

    _____

    _____

    _____

    _____

    _____

    _____

    _____

    _____

    _____

12. Events at the race change Squeaky's view of Raymond.

   • In what way does Squeaky see her brother differently?
   • How will Squeaky's new view of Raymond affect the two of them in the future?

   Use information from the story to support your response.

_____   _____

_____   _____

_____   _____

_____   _____

_____   _____

_____   _____

_____   _____

_____   _____

_____   _____

_____   _____

LANGUAGE ARTS LITERACY: PART 5

Writing Situation: The amount of homework assigned to students seems to increase each year. Many students and parents believe that the workload has become too great, especially in Grades 10 and 11. They say that homework is of questionable value and takes away time from students' extracurricular activities. They propose a change in school policy. They want teachers to assign little—or no—homework. However, other students and parents, as well as teachers and administrators, strongly disagree. They insist that homework serves many sound educational purposes. The proposal has become a controversial issue.

You've decided to write a letter to the school principal expressing your opinions about this issue. What is your point of view? How would the proposed change in school policy on homework affect you and other students in your school?

Writing Task: Write a letter to the principal either supporting or opposing the proposed change in school policy regarding homework. Use facts, examples, and other evidence to support your point of view.

LANGUAGE ARTS LITERACY: PART 1

Writing Task: It's often said that a picture is worth a thousand words. Regardless of an artist's or photographer's intent, what one person sees in a picture may be very different from what others see.

How would you describe what is happening in this picture? Use your imagination and your experience to speculate about the events.

_____

_____

_____

_____

_____

_____

_____

_____

_____

LANGUAGE ARTS LITERACY: PART 2

Directions: Read the selection and answer the questions that follow.

When faced with a challenging opportunity, we can choose to accept it or not. In the following essay, writer James Lincoln Collier discusses how he learned to react to such opportunities.

Anxiety: Challenge by Another Name
by James Lincoln Collier

Between my sophomore and junior years at college, a chance came up for me to spend the summer vacation working on a ranch in Argentina. My roommate's father was in the cattle business, and he wanted Ted to see something of it. Ted said he would go if he could take a friend, and he chose me.

2 The idea of spending two months on the fabled Argentine Pampas[1] was exciting. Then I began having second thoughts. I had never been very far from New England, and I had been homesick my first weeks at college. What would it be like in a strange country? What about the language? And besides, I had promised to teach my younger brother to sail that summer. The more I thought about it, the more the prospect daunted me. I began waking up nights in a sweat.

In the end I turned down the proposition. As soon as Ted asked somebody else to go, I began kicking myself. A couple of weeks later I went home to my old summer job, unpacking cartons at the local supermarket, feeling very low. I had turned down something I wanted to do because I was scared, and had ended up feeling depressed. I stayed that way for a long time. And it didn't help when I went back to college in the fall to discover that Ted and his friend had had a terrific time.

In the long run that unhappy summer taught me a valuable lesson out of which I developed a rule for myself: *do what makes you anxious, don't do what makes you depressed.*

I am not, of course, talking about severe states of anxiety or depression, which require medical attention. What I mean is that kind of anxiety we call stage fright, butterflies in the stomach, a case of nerves—the feelings we have at a job interview, when we're giving a big party, when we have to make an important presentation at the office. And the kind of depression I am referring to is that down-hearted feeling of the blues, when we don't seem to be interested in anything, when we can't get going and seem to have no energy.

I was confronted by this sort of situation toward the end of my senior year. As graduation approached, I began to think about taking a crack at making my living as a writer. But one of my professors was urging me to apply to graduate school and aim at a teaching career.

7 I wavered. The idea of trying to live by writing was scary—a lot more scary than spending a summer on the Pampas, I thought. Back and forth I went, making my decision, unmaking it. Suddenly, I realized that every time I gave up the idea of writing, that sinking feeling went through me; it gave me the blues.

The thought of graduate school wasn't what depressed me. It was giving up on what deep in my gut I really wanted to do. Right then I learned another lesson. To avoid that kind of depression meant, inevitably, having to endure a certain amount of worry and concern.

The great Danish philosopher Soren Kierkegaard believed that anxiety always arises when we confront the possibility of our own development. It seems to be a rule of life that you can't advance without getting that old, familiar, jittery feeling.

10 Even as children we discover this when we try to expand ourselves by, say, learning to ride a bike or going out for the school play. Later in life we get butterflies when we think about having that first child, or uprooting the family from the old hometown to find a better opportunity halfway across the country. Any time, it seems, that we set out aggressively to get something we want, we meet up with anxiety. And it's going to be our traveling companion, at least part of the way, into any new venture.

When I first began writing magazine articles, I was frequently required to interview big names—people like Richard Burton, Joan Rivers, sex authority William Mas-

[1]Grassy plains in South America.

ters, baseball great Dizzy Dean. Before each interview I would get butterflies and my hands would shake.

At the time, I was doing some writing about music. And one person I particularly admired was the great composer Duke Ellington. On stage and on television, he seemed the very model of the confident, sophisticated man of the world. Then I learned that Ellington still got stage fright. If the highly honored Duke Ellington, who had appeared on the bandstand some ten thousand times over thirty years, had anxiety attacks, who was I to think I could avoid them?

I went on doing those frightening interviews, and one day, as I was getting onto a plane for Washington to interview columnist Joseph Alsop, I suddenly realized to my astonishment that I was looking forward to the meeting. What had happened to those butterflies?

Well, in truth, they were still there, but there were fewer of them. I had benefited, I discovered, from a process psychologists call "extinction." If you put an individual in an anxiety-provoking situation often enough, he will eventually learn that there isn't anything to be worried about.

Which brings us to a corollary to my basic rule: *you'll never eliminate anxiety by avoiding the things that caused it.* I remember how my son Jeff was when I first began to teach him to swim at the lake cottage where we spent our summer vacations. He resisted, and when I got him into the water he sank and sputtered and wanted to quit. But I was insistent. And by summer's end he was splashing around like a puppy. He had "extinguished" his anxiety the only way he could—by confronting it.

The problem, of course, is that it is one thing to urge somebody else to take on these anxiety-producing challenges; it is quite another to get ourselves to do it.

Some years ago I was offered a writing assignment that would require three months of travel through Europe. I had been abroad a couple of times on the usual "If it's Tuesday this must be Belgium" trips, but I hardly could claim to know my way around the continent. Moreover, my knowledge of foreign languages was limited to a little college French.

I hesitated. How would I, unable to speak the language, totally unfamiliar with local geography or transportation systems, set up interviews and do research? It seemed impossible, and with considerable regret I sat down to write a letter begging off. Halfway through, a thought—which I subsequently made into another corollary to my basic rule—ran through my mind: *you can't learn if you don't try.* So I accepted the assignment.

There were some bad moments. But by the time I had finished the trip I was an experienced traveler. And ever since, I have never hesitated to head for even the most exotic of places, without guides or even advanced bookings, confident that somehow I will manage.

The point is that the new, the different, is almost by definition scary. But each time you try something, you learn, and as the learning piles up, the world opens to you. **20**

I've made parachute jumps, learned to ski at 40, flown up the Rhine in a balloon. And I know I'm going to go on doing such things. It's not because I'm braver or more daring than others. I'm not. But I don't let the butterflies stop me from doing what I want. Accept anxiety as another name for challenge and you can accomplish wonders.

1. What is the central idea of this selection?

   A. It is wise to avoid unnecessary risks.
   B. Don't let your fear of new experiences hold you back.
   C. Some people are braver than others.
   D. It is foolish to feel nervous about meeting a challenge.

2. The author learned that

   A. only people without confidence experience anxiety.
   B. depression is part of accepting a challenge.
   C. anxiety leads to depression.
   D. avoiding depression meant accepting some anxiety.

3. The author's tone can best be described as

   A. sincere and encouraging.
   B. depressed and cynical.
   C. cautious and uncertain.
   D. annoyed and impatient.

4. When the author refers to the psychological process of "extinction," he means

   A. paying no attention to our anxieties.
   B. eliminating anxiety by facing it.
   C. avoiding activities that cause anxiety.
   D. learning to enjoy unpleasant activities.

5. The author believes that anxiety is

    A. a character flaw.
    B. part of personal growth.
    C. the result of depression.
    D. a problem of the young.

6. What advice would the author be most likely to give?

    A. Be open to new experiences even if they make you nervous.
    B. Play it safe by avoiding challenges.
    C. Never take on a task if you're not sure you can do it.
    D. Avoid anxiety-causing experiences until later in life.

7. As used in paragraph 2, the word **fabled** means

    A. not real.
    B. cold.
    C. famous.
    D. mountainous.

8. In paragraph 10, the author writes that when "we set out aggressively to get something we want, we meet up with anxiety. And it's going to be our traveling companion . . . into any new venture." This is an example of

    A. symbolism.
    B. elaboration.
    C. hyperbole.
    D. personification.

9. The word **wavered** in paragraph 7 means

    A. decided.
    B. disagreed.
    C. hesitated.
    D. trembled.

10. The three-month writing assignment in Europe was significant for the author because it

    A. gave him confidence in his abilities.
    B. taught him that it was okay to fail.
    C. proved that there is nothing scary about new experiences.
    D. made him realize that he had more courage than other people.

OPEN-ENDED ITEM

11. Missing out on the summer in Argentina taught the author to "do what makes you anxious, don't do what makes you depressed."

    • Explain what the author means by this statement.
    • How might following this advice help someone make a difficult decision?

    Use information from the selection to support your response.

    _____

    _____

    _____

    _____

    _____

    _____

    _____

    _____

    _____

    _____

    _____

    _____

    _____

    _____

12. In paragraph 20, the author writes: ". . . each time you try something, you learn, and as the learning piles up, the world opens up to you."

    • What does the author mean by "the world opens up to you"?
    • How might a young person benefit from having his/her world "open up"?

Use information from the selection to support your response.

_____

_____

_____

_____

_____

_____

_____

_____

_____

_____

_____

_____

_____

_____

_____

_____

_____

_____

_____

LANGUAGE ARTS LITERACY: PART 3

Writing: Revise/Edit

Many television programs and movies contain violence, sexual content, drug use, and/or objectionable language. A growing number of people are demanding that access to such shows and movies be controlled or restricted.

One of your classmates has written an essay for the school newspaper expressing his views on this controversial issue and has asked you to revise and edit his first draft. Read the draft, and think about how to improve and clarify the text. Then make your revisions.

Television programs and movies these days have something to offend everyone theres violence, drug use, bad language, and many other kinds of offensive stuff of all sorts. Yet, most programs and movies are readily accessible. To viewers of all ages.

People is demanding that access to objectionable material be controled. Or restricted. These people are 100 percent right. There's no reason in the whole wide world that a child or even a teenager they need to be exposed to things many adults find is offensive

Kids immitate what they see and hear. Watching violence, sex, and drug use puts bad ideas in there minds, just imagine how many young people have gotten in trouble by trying something that looked real "cool" on TV or in the movies.

the surest way to keep TV shows and movies from negatively influence young viewers are to limmit what they can be watching. There is lots of ways how.

First, certain content should simply be banned from TV and movies. At the very least, violence, bad language, and the like should be kept of the air. Till late at night, when most kids were asleeping.

Second, the making of truly worthless offensive shows should be prohibbitted by law. there would be no more "slasher" movies for example. All they do is show blood, gore, and multaple murders.

Third, all TV shows and movies should be rated and restricted. Age-appropriate only can see. Parents should strictly limit what their childrens viewing to suitible shows. Teenagers shouldn't not be allowed to see R-rated movies. Or rent them at video stores neither, this restrictshun seemed to be seldom enforced unfortunately

it won't be easy controlling what viewers can and cannot be watching or not watching but if doing that means protecting young people from bad stuff then the efort surely is worth it for sure

LANGUAGE ARTS LITERACY: PART 4

Directions: Read the selection and answer the questions that follow.

Sometimes a person can accomplish a long sought-after goal in an unexpected way. The following story explores this idea through the interaction of three characters.

The Last Leaf
by O. Henry

In a little district west of Washington Square the streets have run crazy and broken themselves into small strips called "places." These "places" make strange angles and curves. One street crosses itself a time or two. An artist once discovered a valuable possibility in this street. Suppose a collector with a bill for paints, paper and canvas should, in traversing this route, suddenly meet himself coming back, without a cent having been paid on account!

So, to quaint old Greenwich Village the art people soon came prowling, hunting for north windows and eighteenth-century gables and Dutch attics and low rents. Then they imported some pewter mugs and a chafing dish or two from Sixth Avenue, and became a "colony."

At the top of a squatty, three-story brick Sue and Johnsy had their studio. "Johnsy" was familiar for Joanna. One was from Maine, the other from California. They had met at the *table d'hôte* of an Eighth Street "Delmonico's," and found their tastes in art, chicory salad and bishop sleeves so congenial that the joint studio resulted.

That was in May. In November a cold, unseen stranger, whom the doctors called Pneumonia, stalked about the **4** colony, touching one here and there with his icy fingers. Over the east side this ravager strode boldly, smiting his victims by scores, but his feet trod slowly through the maze of the narrow and moss-grown "places."

Mr. Pneumonia was not what you would call a chivalric old gentleman. A mite of a little woman with blood thinned by California zephyrs[1] was hardly fair game for the red-fisted, short-breathed old duffer. But Johnsy he smote; and she lay, scarcely moving, on her painted iron bedstead, looking through the small Dutch window-panes at the blank side of the next brick house.

One morning the busy doctor invited Sue into the hallway with a shaggy, gray eyebrow.

"She has one chance in—let us say ten," he said, as he shook down the mercury in his clinical thermometer. "And that chance is for her to want to live. This way people have of lining-up on the side of the undertaker makes **7** the entire pharmacopoeia look silly. Your little lady has made up her mind that she's not going to get well. Has she anything on her mind?"

"She—she wanted to paint the Bay of Naples some day," said Sue.

"Paint?—bosh! Has she anything on her mind worth thinking about twice—a man for instance?"

"A man?" said Sue, with a jew's-harp twang in her voice. "Is a man worth—but, no doctor; there is nothing of the kind."

"Well, it is the weakness, then," said the doctor, "I will do all that science, so far as it may filter through my efforts, can accomplish. But whenever my patient begins to count the carriages in her funeral procession I subtract 50 percent from the curative power of medicines. If you will get her back to ask one question about the new winter styles in cloak sleeves I will promise you a one-in-five chance for her, instead of one in ten."

After the doctor had gone Sue went into the workroom and cried a Japanese napkin to a pulp. Then she swaggered **12** into Johnsy's room with her drawing board, whistling ragtime.

Johnsy lay, scarcely making a ripple under the bedclothes, with her face toward the window. Sue stopped whistling, thinking she was asleep.

She arranged her board and began a pen-and-ink drawing to illustrate a magazine story. Young artists must pave their way to Art by drawing pictures for magazine stories that young authors write to pave their way to Literature.

[1]Warm breezes

As Sue was sketching a pair of elegant horseshow riding trousers and a monocle on the figure of the hero, an Idaho cowboy, she heard a low sound, several times repeated. She went quickly to the bedside.

Johnsy's eyes were open wide. She was looking out the window and counting—counting backward.

"Twelve," she said, and a little later, "eleven"; and then "ten," and "nine"; and then "eight" and "seven," almost together.

Sue looked <u>solicitously</u> out of the window. What was there to count? There was only a bare, dreary yard to be seen, and the blank side of the brick house twenty feet away. An old, old ivy vine, gnarled and decayed at the roots, climbed half way up the brick wall. The cold breath of autumn had stricken its leaves from the vine until its skeleton branches clung, almost bare, to the crumbling bricks.

"What is it, dear?" asked Sue.

"Six," said Johnsy, in almost a whisper. "They're falling faster now. Three days ago there were almost a hundred. It made my head ache to count them, But now it's easy. There goes another one. There are only five left now."

"Five what, dear? Tell your Sudie."

"Leaves. On the ivy vine. When the last one falls I must go, too. I've known that for three days. Didn't the doctor tell you?"

"Oh, I never heard of such nonsense," complained Sue, with magnificent scorn. "What have old ivy leaves to do with your getting well? And you used to love that vine so, you naughtly girl. Don't be a goosey. Why, the doctor told me this morning that your chances for getting well real soon were—let's see exactly what he said—he said the chances were ten to one! Why, that's almost as good a chance as we have in New York when we ride on the street cars or walk past a new building. Try to take some broth now, and let Sudie go back to her drawing, so she can sell the editor man with it, and buy port wine for her sick child, and pork chops for her greedy self."

"You needn't get any more wine," said Johnsy, keeping her eyes fixed out the window. "There goes another. No, I don't want any broth. That leaves just four. I want to see the last one fall before it gets dark. Then I'll go, too."

"Johnsy, dear," said Sue, bending over her, "will you promise me to keep your eyes closed, and not look out the window until I am done working? I must hand those drawings in by tomorrow. I need the light, or I would draw the shade down."

"Couldn't you draw in the other room?" asked Johnsy, coldly.

"I'd rather be here by you," said Sue. "Besides, I don't want you to keep looking at those silly ivy leaves."

"Tell me as soon as you have finished," said Johnsy, closing her eyes, and lying white and still as a fallen statue, "because I want to see the last one fall. I'm tired of waiting. I'm tired of thinking. I want to turn loose my hold on everything and go sailing down, down, just like one of those poor, tired leaves."

"Try to sleep," said Sue. "I must call Behrman up to be my model for the old hermit miner. I'll not be gone a minute! Don't try to move 'til I come back."

Old Behrman was a painter who lived on the ground floor beneath them. He was past sixty and had a Michael Angelo's Moses beard curling down from the head of a satyr along the body of an imp. Behrman was a failure in art. Forty years he had wielded the brush without getting near enough to touch the hem of his Mistress's robe. He had been always about to paint a masterpiece, but had never yet begun it. For several years he had painted nothing except now and then a daub in the line of commerce or advertising. He earned a little by serving as a model to those young artists in the colony who could not pay the price of a professional. He drank gin to excess, and still talked of his coming masterpiece. For the rest he was a fierce little old man, who scoffed terribly at softness in any one, and who regarded himself as especial mastiff-in-waiting to protect the two young artists in the studio above.

Sue found Behrman smelling strongly of juniper berries in his dimly lighted den below. In one corner was a blank canvas on an easel that had been waiting there for twenty-five years to receive the first line of the masterpiece. She told him of Johnsy's fancy, and how she feared she would, indeed, light and fragile as a leaf herself, float away, when her slight hold upon the world grew weaker.

Old Behrman, with his red eyes plainly streaming, shouted his contempt and <u>derision</u> for such idiotic imaginings.

"Vass!" he cried, "Is dere people in de world mit der foolishness to die because leafs dey drop off from a confounded vine? I haf not heard of such a thing. No, I will not bose as a model for your fool hermit-dunderhead. Vy do you allow dot silly pusiness to come in der brain of her? Ach, dot poor leetle Miss Yohnsy."

"She is very ill and weak," said Sue, "and the fever has left her mind morbid and full of strange fancies. Very well, Mr. Behrman, if you do not care to pose for me, you needn't. But I think you are a horrid old—old flibbertigibbet."

"You are just like a woman!" yelled Behrman. "Who said I will not bose? Go on, I come mit you. For half an hour I haf peen trying to say dot I am ready to bose. Gott! dis is not any blace in which one so goot as Miss Yohnsy shall lie sick. Some day I vill baint a masterpiece, and ve shall all go away. Gott! yes."

Johnsy was sleeping when they went up-stairs. Sue pulled the shade down to the window-sill, and motioned Behrman into the other room. In there they peered out the window fearfully at the ivy vine. Then they looked at each other for a moment without speaking. A persistent, cold rain was falling, min-gled with snow. Behrman, in his old blue shirt, took his seat as the hermit miner on an upturned kettle for a rock.

When Sue awoke from an hour's sleep the next morning she found Johnsy with dull, wide-open eyes staring at the drawn green shade.

"Pull it up; I want to see," she ordered, in a whisper.

Wearily Sue obeyed.

But, lo! After the beating rain and fierce gusts of wind that had endured through the livelong night, there yet stood out against the brick wall one ivy leaf. It was the last on the vine. Still dark green near its stem, but with its serrated edges tinted with the yellow of dissolution and decay, it hung bravely from a branch some twenty feet above the ground.

"It is the last one," said Johnsy. "I thought it would surely fall during the night. I heard the wind. It will fall to-day, and I shall die at the same time."

"Dear, dear!" said Sue, leaning her worn face down the pillow, "think of me, if you won't think of yourself. What would I do?"

But Johnsy did not answer. The lonesomest thing in all the world is a soul when it is making ready to go on its mysterious, far journey. The fancy seemed to possess her more strongly as one by one the ties that bound her to friendship and to earth were loosed.

The day wore away, and even though the twilight they could see the lone ivy leaf clinging to its stem against the wall. And then, with the coming of the night the north wind was again loosed, while the rain still beat against the windows and pattered down from the low Dutch eaves.

When it was light enough Johnsy, the merciless, com-manded that the shade be raised.

The ivy leaf was still there.

Johnsy lay for a long time looking at it. And then she called to Sue, who was stirring her chicken broth over the gas stove.

"I've been a bad girl, Sudie," said Johnsy. "Some-thing has made that the last leaf stay there to show me how wicked I was. It is a sin to want to die. You may bring me a little broth now, and some milk with a little port in it, and —no; bring me a hand-mirror first, and then pack some pillows about me, and I will sit up and watch you cook."

An hour later she said:

"Sudie, some day I hope to paint the Bay of Naples."

The doctor came in the afternoon, and Sue had an excuse to go into the hallway as he left.

"Even chances," said the doctor, taking Sue's thin, shak-ing hand in his. "With good nursing you'll win. And now I must see another case I have downstairs. Behrman, his name is—some kind of an artist, I believe. Pneumonia, too. He is an old, weak man, and the attack is acute. There is no hope for him, but he goes to the hospital to-day to be made more comfortable."

The next day the doctor said to Sue: "She's out of danger. You've won. Nutrition and care now—that's all."

And that afternoon Sue came to the bed where Johnsy lay, contentedly knitting a very blue and very useless woollen shoulder scarf, and put one arm around her, pillows and all.

"I have something to tell you, white mouse," she said, "Mr. Behrman died of pneumonia to-day in the hospital. He was ill only two days. The janitor found him on the morning of the first day in his room downstairs helpless with pain. His shoes and clothing were wet through and icy cold. They couldn't imagine where he had been on such a dreadful night. And then they found a lantern, still lighted, and a ladder that had been dragged from its place, and some scattered brushes, and a palette with green and yellow colors mixed on it, and—look out the window, dear, at the last ivy leaf on the wall. Didn't you wonder why it never fluttered or moved when the wind blew? Ah, darling, it's Behrman's masterpiece—he painted it there the night that the last leaf fell."

1. Why are the leaves on the ivy vine significant?

   A. Sue was drawing them for a magazine story.
   B. They symbolize the change of seasons.
   C. Behrman always wanted to paint them.
   D. Johnsy thought she would die when the last leaf fell.

2. In paragraph 18, Sue looks "**solicitously** out of the window." In this context, **solicitously** means

   A. with concern.
   B. with amusement.
   C. indifferently.
   D. angrily.

3. In paragraph 7, the doctor refers to people "lining-up on the side of the undertaker." This is an example of

   A. simile.
   B. metaphor.
   C. alliteration.
   D. foreshadowing.

4. In paragraph 12, the author writes: "After the doctor had gone Sue went into the workroom and cried a Japanese napkin to a pulp. Then she swaggered into Johnsy's room with her drawing board, whistling ragtime." The purpose of this paragraph is to show that

   A. Sue has decided to ignore what the doctor said.
   B. Sue has mixed feelings about Johnsy's condition.
   C. Ragtime music is Sue's favorite.
   D. Sue wants to hide the seriousness of the situation.

5. In paragraph 32, Behrman "shouted his contempt and **derision**." In this context, **derision** means

   A. respect.
   B. ridicule.
   C. curiosity.
   D. admiration.

6. At the beginning, the doctor gives Johnsy poor odds for recovery mainly because Johnsy

   A. has lost the will to live.
   B. refuses to take her medicine.
   C. has a fatal illness.
   D. is very old.

7. In paragraph 4, the author describes the effects of an "unseen stranger." In this paragraph, the author is using a literary device called

   A. hyperbole.
   B. personification.
   C. oxymoron.
   D. allegory.

8. In the final sentence, why does Sue refer to the leaf on the wall as "Behrman's masterpiece"?

   A. It was an outstanding painting of a leaf.
   B. It was a valuable work of art.
   C. It was his greatest work because it saved Johnsy's life.
   D. It was the last painting Behrman did before he died.

9. The most likely reason why Behrman painted the leaf is because

   A. Sue asked him to.
   B. he was concerned about Johnsy.
   C. he wanted to create a masterpiece.
   D. the doctor suggested it.

10. Behrman died because he

    A. caught pneumonia from Johnsy.
    B. fell off a ladder while painting.
    C. painted the leaf during a cold and rainy night.
    D. was heartbroken at the thought of losing Johnsy.

OPEN-ENDED ITEM

11. People's actions and feelings affect the lives of those around them.

    • How did Behrman's actions affect the lives of all three main characters, including his own?
    • If *any* of the main characters had behaved differently, the story might have unfolded in a very different way. Explain.

    Use information from the story to support your response.

    _____

    _____

    _____

    _____

_____

_____

_____

_____

_____

_____

_____

_____

_____

_____

_____

_____

_____

_____

12. Characters, like people, are more complex than they first seem.

- Behrman is first described as "a failure in art" and "a fierce little old man." To what extent is this description accurate?
- After Behrman's death, how are Sue and Johnsy likely to describe him?

Use information from the story to support your response.

_____

_____

_____

_____

_____

_____

_____

_____

_____

_____

_____

_____

_____

_____

_____

_____

_____

_____

_____

_____

LANGUAGE ARTS LITERACY: PART 5

Writing Situation: Some state legislators insist that parents are largely to blame for the actions of their teenagers. They say, for example, that parents who leave their teens alone too much make it easy for them to get into trouble. These legislators are demanding that parents be held legally responsible if their teenager is caught drinking beer, driving recklessly, shoplifting, or doing anything else seriously wrong. They also want parents penalized if a party gets out of hand while they are not home and the police come. However, other legislators believe that punishing parents for what their teens do would be unfair. The issue has become a controversial one in the legislature.

Your English teacher has asked students to write an essay explaining their opinions about this issue. What is your point of view? How might the proposed legal penalties for parents affect you, other teenagers, and families?

Writing Task: Write an essay either supporting or opposing the proposed legal penalties for parents. Use facts, examples, and other evidence to support your point of view.

INDEX